What

MW00909291

United and Ignited

Wow! Dennis has given the Church a very significant gift! It is a rare church that has not struggled with both the concept and the practice of corporate prayer. This book is going to help in both areas. It is unique in building its structure around *The QUESTions* that pastors and church leaders have been (or should be) asking. I see a new wave of prayer coming as a result of *United and Ignited.*

– Dave Butts
Chairman, America's National Prayer Committee
President, Harvest Prayer Ministries, Terra Haute, Indiana

I have several shelves of books on prayer in my office. Most of them address private prayer, the theology of prayer, the need for prayer. *United and Ignited* by my friend, Dennis Fuqua, is a much needed, how-to book on corporate prayer. Reading it brings joy. Adding it to my collection brings balance. Recommending it brings pleasure. Add it to your reading list. Incorporate it into your prayer groups, families, churches. The leader has much to learn from this book. The family of God has much to gain from leaders reading and applying the principles and practices of this book.

– Dr. Dan R. Crawford
Senior Professor of Evangelism & Missions, Chair of Prayer Emeritus, Southwestern Baptist Theological Seminary, Fort Worth, Texas
President, Disciple All Nations, Inc.

Don't read this book... unless you are ready and eager for a different kind of prayer experience. This book is the GPS for your journey into dynamic *corporate* prayer. Dennis is a pioneer who has both the skills and spiritual sensitivity necessary to explain and train you to lead small groups or large gatherings into an authentic encounter with God.

–Phil Miglioratti
Facilitator of *Pray!* Network, Palatine, Illinois

Dynamic, corporate prayer is changing my life, my church and my city. Practical, balanced and utilizing wisdom garnered through thousands of hours of prayer facilitation - *United and Ignited* encourages leaders in our churches and cities to facilitate profound prayer experiences. Andrew Murray has stated, "The man who mobilizes the Christian church to pray will make the greatest contribution to world evangelization in history". Dennis, through *United and Ignited,* is discipling world-changing prayer mobilizers. Let's read it, use it, live it - and may His Kingdom come as we do!

– Kevin Moore
Executive Director, Mission Birmingham
Worship and Outreach Pastor, Shades Mountain Independent Church, Birmingham, Alabama

Dennis has created a much needed resource for church leaders, council members, worship team members and worship planners. The style of the book is engaging and the format is easy to use. For anyone wanting a nuts and bolts guide to the foundational issues around facilitating corporate prayer, this book is for you.

–J Scott Roberts
Pastor, Hope in Christ Church
Bellingham, Washington

I am thrilled Dennis has finally put on paper what he has been modeling and teaching many pastors and prayer facilitators for many years, and that is; *How to effectively lead a corporate prayer meeting while broadening people's understanding of Scriptural based, personal and corporate prayer.*

Fuqua's approach to prayer, especially leading corporate prayer, is rich, warm and engaging to both the seasoned prayer warrior and the new believer. I highly recommend and endorse *United and*

Ignited as a "must have" resource for all pastors and ministry leaders who are committed to strong biblical discipleship – helping their congregants to "*Continue steadfastly in prayer, being watchful in it with thanks-giving.*" Colossians 4:2

–Ezra Okoti
Prayer and Discipleship Ministries
Northview Community Church, Abbotsford, BC

Books on prayer can be notorious for being boring, or setting folks to snoring. I know Dennis to be a man authentically passionate about the practice of corporate prayer. *United and Ignited* offers creative ideas for divine conversations that have emerged from the crucible of a variety of intercessory encounters. This is not your standard, re-warmed bread. This is fresh-baked manna that will nourish any soul hungry for a deeper, more satisfying engagement in community prayer. Dennis offers up a variety of practical, ready-to-use tools. I commend this book to any and all who facilitate group prayer.

–Tom White
Founder/President
Frontline Ministries, Corvallis, Oregon

Here is an excellent practical guide for the prayer facilitator. Whether one is relatively new or broadly experienced in leading corporate prayer, this book contains a wealth of wise insights to prepare and lead group prayer. It is immersed in the biblical text and well organized for present use and future study. I warmly endorse and widely recommend *United and Ignited* as a guidebook and resource for corporate prayer. It is a tool designed to serve us as we endeavor to serve others in the sacred task of united prayer.

–Rob Wiggins
Dean of Student Development
Western Seminary, Portland, Oregon

UNITED *AND* IGNITED

Encountering God *through*
Dynamic Corporate Prayer

DENNIS FUQUA

UNITED AND IGNITED
© 2012 Dennis Fuqua
www.uandibook.net

Published by
L/P Press
Vancouver, WA. USA
www.livingprayer.net

International Standard Book Number
ISBN-13:
978-1478177777

ISBN-10:
1478177772

Cover design by Vinnie Kinsella at Indigo Editing and Publishing with
help from Kristin Paul Design.

Forward

I've had the privilege of participating in several *Prayer Summits* that Dennis Fuqua facilitated. I have been amazed at his ability to foster good group prayer. Several times during his sessions I said to myself, "Dennis is so good at leading group prayer, I wish he would put what he has learned in a book." Well he did! And here it is— *United and Ignited, Encountering God through Dynamic Corporate Prayer.* You will find that it's well written and richly insightful.

United and Ignited is a one-of-a-kind book on prayer. I have about five hundred books on prayer in my library, but this book is unlike any other prayer book on my shelves. It starts with a clear definition of dynamic corporate prayer; goes on to spell out clearly the role of the facilitator; then delineates how these principles can be incorporated into the life of a local congregation and even in families. What makes this volume so unique is that it spells out the why and how of prayer leadership down to the most practical levels.

There is a huge need for this book today. The revival that many spiritual leaders long for and pray for will not happen without corporate prayer. Corporate prayer will not flourish unless pastors take the lead. Pastors will not take the lead unless they are well trained. Very few of us pastors have been adequately trained in the principles and practices of corporate prayer. But with this volume in their hands, many pastors will be able to give their congregations the necessary leadership to develop dynamic corporate prayer. That will lay the foundation for revival in the church.

I have had the privilege of knowing and praying with Dennis for many years. I know of no prayer leader in North America who is more qualified to write on corporate prayer than Dennis Fuqua. His book has been forged out of years of experience on the front lines of prayer ministry. He has been the director of

International Renewal Ministries since 2000. In that position he regularly facilitates *Pray-er Summits* around the nation and around the world and, in addition, leads prayer seminars based on his book *Living Prayer.* His per-sonal stories and how-to-do-it experiential insights are invaluable.

If, in picking up this book, you are looking for real-life answers to your real-life questions about corporate prayer you won't be disappointed. Do you want to know the primary components of dynamic corporate prayer? You'll find them here. Are you curious about the role of the Holy Spirit in corporate prayer? You'll discover that in this volume. Do you wonder if corporate prayer can revive your church's weekly prayer meeting? You will learn from *United and Ignited* why and how it can. This book answered every question I ever asked about corporate prayer. I think it will answer your questions too.

I am glad that you have been drawn to this book. As you read, grasp, and apply the principles and practices recommended in these pages, you will find yourself leading corporate prayer in a way you never thought possible. *It has the potential to revolutionize the way that prayer is perceived and experienced in the life of any local church, including yours.*

In response to reading this volume, I encourage you to do three things. First, pray about prayer. Yes, pray about prayer! Pray that God will teach you about prayer from his Word as well as through this volume. Pray that you will be able to pray like Jesus and intercede like Paul. Pray that your church will become as devoted to prayer as the first Church of Jerusalem was (Acts 1:14, 2:42, 4:24, 6:4). Pray that you will have a growing love and ability to facilitate corporate prayer.

Second, practice these principles by facilitating prayer every chance you get. Create opportunities for people to come together in prayer, and then step up to facilitate these prayer times. A leadership skill that is used will grow strong.

Third, train others to lead corporate prayer. Multiplying the number of skilled prayer facilitators is bound to increase the amount of corporate prayer and the number of prayer-devoted churches. That's what you really want isn't it?

Dr. Alvin VanderGriend,
Prayer Evangelism Associate for Harvest Prayer Ministries

The "QUESTions"

5

7

9

Prelude – What should I know about this book?

1. How can I get the most out of this book?

This book is designed to be a tool. A tool you can use to move people closer to the Lord. A tool you can use to help build them up in their faith. It is a tool for prayer; a tool to both encourage you and equip you to help others encounter Jesus Christ through prayer.

It is formatted around questions. Learning how to facilitate group prayer that impacts the lives of the pray-ers is a quest, a journey. Hence, *The QUESTions*. Some are questions I have been asked. Some are questions I have anticipated. The questions fall under larger categories or Sections. It is formatted in this way to help you go directly to the questions you would like to pursue. Of course, it is designed to be read from beginning to end, but more than that it is designed to be referred to again and again.

I would encourage you to start by reading all *The QUESTions* so you get a sense of the overall flow of the book. I have arranged the questions in what I consider to be a logical sequence. But, if you are interested in specific topics, you are welcome to go directly to those topics. In essence you can follow your own path. I have tried to make each question be able to stand alone, so there is some material repeated from question to question.

But *reading* this book is not the way you can get the most out of it. *Doing* what is written here is. The reason I have given so many illustrations is to help you get a picture of how you can facilitate this type of prayer. This is also the reason for the *blessed by doing* sections at key points in the book. The truth of John 13:17 [Now that you know these things, you will be blessed if you do

> **Improve upon what I have written. Experiment. Risk. Be stretched. Stretch others.**

them.] can be applied universally. Once you know a certain truth about facilitating corporate prayer, the real blessing to you and others comes when you actually do it. So, I encourage you to make or take as many opportunities as possible to follow the suggestions here as you learn to lead others in prayer. These sections are marked like this…

 ➢ **Blessed by Doing** –

Finally, don't be satisfied with what you read here. See this as a journey. Keep at it. Keep asking the Lord how He wants you to lead times of prayer. Improve upon what I have written. Experiment. Risk. Be stretched. Stretch others. Listen to God's directions and follow them. Just as the blessing is in the doing, the best blessings come from doing this over a long period of time.

2. **What are some examples of prayer that resulted in people being *united* and *ignited*?**

Location: Jerusalem.
Date: C. 32 AD.
People: Jerusalem believers with Peter and John.
Scripture: Acts 4:23-31.
Setting: Peter and John report about being threatened by the religious leaders to no longer speak or minister in Jesus' name.
Activity: Fervent, united, corporate prayer.
Result: The place where they prayed was shaken, they were filled with the Holy Spirit, they were bold in their witness.

Location: Jerusalem.
Date: C. 44 AD.
People: Disciples minus James and Peter
Scripture: Acts 12:1-19
Settings: Herod had just killed James. It looked like Peter would be

next.

Activity: No recorded prayer for James, but earnest, corporate prayer for Peter.

Result: Peter's amazing, angelic deliverance from prison. The church turned from unbelief to astonishment.

Location: Antioch.
Date: C. 46 AD.
People: leaders of the Church at Antioch
Scripture: Acts 13:1-3.
Setting: leaders set time aside to spend with the Lord with no known agenda.
Activity: Passionate corporate worship and prayer.
Result: The Holy Spirit spoke. They obeyed. The missionary advance of the church to 'the ends of the earth" began. It has never stopped.

Location: Hernhut, Germany
Date: August 13, 1727
People: The Moravians; a struggling Christian community of believers led by Count Ludwig Von Zinzendorf.
Setting: A rift within the movement threatened its very existence.
Activity: A call to passionate, corporate prayer
Result: Fresh empowerment from the Lord and deep reconciliation within the community that birthed a prayer meeting which lasted over 100 years producing some of the most effective missionary activity since the book of Acts.

Location: Many cities across in USA and other nations
Date: present day
People: Pastors and other spiritual leaders
Setting: Varies from city to city, church to church.
Activity: A fresh level of corporate prayer that is dynamic, attractive.
Result: God encounters. United hearts. Vision ignited. Passion,

perspective, relationship, and mission renewed. More cooperation, less competition. Jesus pleased and proclaimed.
Location: Your church. Your city
Date: 2012 and beyond.
People: You and your friends.
Setting: Will vary from city to city, church to church.
Activity: Fresh, corporate, united, prayer flowing from fresh vision.
Result: God hears and shows up! You can tell us more about what happened later!

In congregations, in ministries, in cities, in Biblical times, throughout history, and today, as people have prayed together the consistent results have been a greater depth of relationship and a greater sense of mission among those who have prayed, and therefore greater impact in their world.

3. What do you mean by *encountering* God?

I seek to understand things from a Biblical world view. When I refer to encountering God, I start with the fact that we live in a universe where the infinite God is also personal. He desires to be known by each person on our planet. This desire to be known is the reason He came to this world in the person of Jesus Christ. Knowing Jesus begins with our acknowledgement that His death on the cross was necessary because we had turned away from Him and His standards. But it does not end there. Knowing Him more and more will be a key part of the life we will enjoy forever. So, in this life – between our surrender to Him and our eternal home with Him – knowing Him is of primary importance.

We know Him more as we encounter Him in some manner. So, when I reference encountering God, I am referring to times which result in a person knowing and enjoying Him more.

The word *encounter* carries several elements with it. There is an element of surprise. We can't plan them, but we can anticipate and respond to them. The word also suggests impact. When we have an encounter with God, we are changed.

Some of these may seem very minor as when I am reminded of His greatness by viewing part of His creation. Some of them may seem much more significant as when He restores part of my broken soul through helping me forgive someone who deeply offended me. These encounters may take place as I read His word or hear it preached, as I ponder His plans, as I appreciate others He has put in my life, or as I sing with others in deep worship.

I have experienced many encounters like this during times of corporate prayer. And I have witnessed many others having similar encounters with Him in the context of corporate prayer. In fact, I have concluded that corporate prayer is an environment where God enjoys encountering us. This is why I have written this book. This is why my prayer is that it will be a great tool for you and others as you seek to facilitate more and better corporate prayer.

> *These encounters may take place as I read His word or hear it preached... or as I sing with others in deep worship.*

4. Why do you use the words *dynamic* and *corporate*?

Dynamic from a dictionary – pertaining to or characterized by energy or effective action; vigorously active and forceful; energetic...
Dynamic from a thesaurus – lively, active, self-motivated, energetic, vibrant, forceful, full of life, vigorous...

Corporate from a dictionary – Pertaining to a united group, as of persons...
Corporate from a thesaurus – shared, group, community, mutual, communal...

Dynamic and *corporate*. This is the kind of prayer that has given me life. I have seen this kind of prayer *unite* and *ignite*. This is the kind of prayer that will give you life. This is the kind of prayer you can use to influence those around you. This is the kind of prayer I want to help you facilitate.

A Google search on the topic of "books on prayer" produced "About 102,000,000 results (in 0.15 seconds)." Yikes! So, there is plenty of material already out there on the vital topic of prayer. How is this book different? Though I don't know the exact percentage, I am sure it is safe to say that the large majority of these books (98%?) deal with the prayer life of the individual, either by way of a biography or a how-to guide. These provide wonderful motivation and instruction on the need to spend personal time in prayer.

This book is not about individual prayer. It is about corporate prayer. Just as God gave us two eyes so we can have depth perception, two ears so we can locate the source of sound, two legs so we can walk and run with balance, and two people in a marriage relationship for better understanding and balance, so also, God has given us the opportunity to pray both individually and with other believers. Vibrant individual prayer and vibrant corporate prayer gives us greater perspective and balance. Scripture says if one of us can put 1,000 to flight, then two of us can conquer 10,000. Praying individually is indispensible. But praying with others adds dimensions to our prayers that cannot come when we are praying by ourselves.

God has given me a unique experience and opportunity. After pastoring a local congregation for 25 years I was asked to become the director of an international prayer ministry. During the 1990's I had the opportunity to attend or facilitate about 20, 3-4 day Pastors' Prayer Summits. Since the turn of the century I have facilitated an average of 15 multiple-day prayer events per year, and hundreds of shorter times of corporate prayer. In these settings God has taught me and allowed me to see His hand at work.

At International Renewal Ministries, we have always desired that those who are blessed at a Pastors' Prayer Summit would "take it back home" to their congregation. Some have, many have not. In recent years I have noticed that as I have facilitated times of prayer some have been taking notes, not only on what has been prayed, but on the process taking place. There is a growing hunger for people to grow in their capacity to help others pray in a more dynamic manner.

Praying individually is indispensible. But praying with others adds dimensions to our prayers that cannot come when we are praying by ourselves.

5. When and where were you first exposed to this kind of prayer?

There are many references to Prayer Summits in this book because for many pastors and spiritual leaders, and those who facilitate dynamic corporate prayer, including myself, our first exposure to it was at a multiple-day Prayer Summit. It is not the only – and may not even be the best – place to experience corporate prayer. But many pastors have commented about how they have never experienced that kind of prayer before. Pastors who attended a Prayer Summit were encouraged to meet together weekly or monthly between their annual Prayer Summits and continue to pray in the same manner but for shorter periods of time.

Some pastors brought it back to their congregations in various ways, such as special evenings or days of prayer, or even incorporating it into their Sunday morning services. As time passed many of us made use of this kind of prayer in many different settings. So, even though in my experience, dynamic corporate prayer was birthed out of the Prayer Summit movement, I am pleased to see it is being used in many other places.

When we set aside a longer time to meet with God, the results seem to be exponential. In fact, my hope is that what you read here will help some of you facilitate more multiple-day Prayer Summits, for pastors and spiritual leaders, for all or part of your congregations or ministries, or for some other group. Why not gather a group of men or women together and challenge them to get away and spend a few days in His presence and see what He might do?

But there is also great value in bringing this style of prayer to many other settings unrelated to a Prayer Summit. So, whether you meet for a few minutes prior to a service, or as a home group, a leadership team, a Sunday School class, a youth group, a group at work, or as a family, what you read here will help enhance your times of praying together.

6. What are your hopes for this book?

The purpose of this book is to help those who desire to lead others in more meaningful corporate prayer find very practical ways to not just *survive* the experience, but to *thrive* because of it. You will find illustrations of how the Lord has led me and others in specific settings, but more importantly you will find principles to follow so you can know how the Lord wants to lead you in your prayer group.

My hope is not that you will be able to reproduce a specific model of prayer, but that you will be able to grow in your own ability and confidence of how the Lord wants to use you to influence others through corporate prayer.

Ultimately, this is a book about a key aspect of *discipleship*. Jesus, in the primary passage on how to make disciples (Matthew 28:19-20), instructs us to teach others all that He has commanded us. One of the things He commanded us to do was to pray. His main instruction on this topic (Matthew 6:9-13) is given in the plural (notice the pronouns "our" and "us"). Paul told Timothy to pass on to others the things he had seen in Paul. Timothy saw Paul pray with others and for others. This was one of the things Paul wanted Timothy to pass on. As we encourage others to pray together, we are encouraging them to be better disciples of Jesus.

So, my hope is that anyone who has spiritual influence in someone else's life, whether as a pastor, a youth pastor, a worship leader, an elder or deacon, a home group leader, a Sunday School

teacher, a co-worker, a fellow student, a fellow-worker, a parent, or a
grand-parent, will find encouragement and help here to assist the
people around them to grow more in
the grace of God available through
corporate prayer.

> *Ultimately, this is a*
> *book about a key*
> *aspect of discipleship.*

7. To whom are you thankful as you have written this book?

I want to express thanks to others who have written on this topic.
Daniel Henderson's books *Fresh Encounters: Experiencing
Transformation through United, Worship-Based Prayer*, as well as
*Transforming Prayer: How Everything Changes When We Seek
God's Face,* and *Prayzing!* have been very helpful to me as has John
Franklin's book *And the Place Was Shaken.*

I am very thankful to Dr. Joe Aldrich, who had a vision of a
united, praying, humble, serving, worshipping Church impacting a
city through dynamic corporate prayer. And to Terry Dirks, who
assisted him in carrying out that vision with such sensitivity and
passion. Dr. Daniel Lockwood and Dr. Richard Palmer, without
your invitation for me to direct International Renewal Ministries I
would not have had the experience or the opportunities necessary to
write this book.

I am also very grateful to those who gave encouragement and
input on this manuscript. Alvin VanderGriend, Daryl Knudeson,
Dick Williams, Glen Weber, Howard Boyd, Jason Hubbard, Jody
Mayhew, Kevin Moore, Phil Miglioratti, Steve Zimmerman, Tim
Klaussen, and Tom White, your input has been extremely helpful to
me. Dan Mayhew, your help with all things technical has accomplished things I could never do. Rob Wiggins, your invitation to
your classroom has helped me think more clearly about how to
move from facilitating prayer to helping others do the same.

Then there is the "too-many-to-mention" category. You may

see some of your great ideas in print here! And I want to thank those who have been so affirming as I have facilitated corporate prayer. Your kind and, at times, frank comments have encouraged me and honed me. I am grateful.

I am also extremely grateful for Marilyn, who has shared life with me in this process. She has not only stood by me, she has also stood by herself as I have been in other places seeking to fulfill God's present assignment for my life. I love you very much.

1 Definitions – What do you mean when you say dynamic corporate prayer?

I remember lying on my face with my head literally underneath the improvised communion table. I don't remember why I went there. I do remember being touched deeply by the Lord as I reflected on the difficulty of the previous three months of ministry. I was aware of the nearly 60 other pastors from my county in the room, but they were not a distraction because most of them were also prostrate before the Lord. I remember the restoration of my soul. I remember the peace that followed. We were pastors from Pierce County, WA. at Cannon Beach, OR. for our first Pastors Prayer Summit.

When I received an invitation to attend it, I was all for it. As a student at Multnomah Biblical Seminary in 1989, I heard the buzz about the very first summit. It struck a chord in my heart. So, when the invitation came about 18 months later from Dr. Joe Aldrich and Terry Dirks, of what was then Northwest Renewal Ministries, I knew I was going.

I was struck by the simplicity of the prayer. How spontaneous, a cappella music helped carry it and merge it with worship. How the Scriptures were not just read, but prayed. How a plan was not always obvious at the beginning of the session, but His plan was obvious by the end of the session. How experienced leaders chose not to lead, but rather be led by the Most Experienced Leader. I had not experienced anything like this before, but I knew I wanted more of it. Individuals were refreshed. As a group we were united. The sessions lasted for hours, but we did not want them to stop. The presence of the Lord will do that to a group.

> *I was struck by the simplicity of the prayer. How spontaneous, a cappella music helped carry it and merge it with worship. How the Scriptures were not just read, but prayed.*

Some of us didn't know each other. Some of us didn't like each other. But as we lingered in His presence, laid down our weapons, listened to each other pour out our hearts, and got to know each other as "staff members of the Church of Pierce County," we couldn't really remember why we didn't either know or like one another much sooner. This was my first exposure to what I now refer to as dynamic corporate prayer.

That may not be the best name. But it is a way of describing the kind of prayer I will share about in this book. Worship-based prayer, or relational prayer, or conversational prayer, or participation prayer, or listening prayer, may be the name you would prefer. I am not as concerned about what you call it as I am that you experience it and help others to experience it. I have settled on the words *dynamic* and *corporate* because I think these two components are essential to its makeup.

Each year for 10 years I attended this annual event. In between, along with four other pastors, we provide leadership for the movement in our county. Soon I facilitated one or two Pastors Prayer Summits per year in other areas. I had no idea that ten years later I would be asked to give leadership to what by then was known as International Renewal Ministries.

1.1 How is it different from a *regular* time of prayer?

To the average person in the pew, prayer is asking God for something or to do something. Most of the praying that takes place in the typical time of prayer has much to do with what we think needs to be changed around us.

I am advocating that, in addition to these regular times of prayer, we also have prayer times when *our* needs are not our primary focus. I am encouraging us to consider prayer that would be more concerned about seeking God's face than seeking His hand. Where the primary focus is on *Him* more than what He might do for *us*. Where we would seek to draw near to Him simply for who He is. Where we would behold *Him* rather than just behold our *circumstances*. And where we would be more interested in His presence than His presents. I am suggesting that there should be times when we follow the pattern of Matthew 6:33. That we seek Him first and anticipate that all the other things we really need would be added to us because we have sought Him first.

Generally speaking there seems to be no difference in our individual prayers and when we are praying with others. I am advocating for a kind of prayer that is more dependent upon *listening* than it is upon *lists*. A kind of prayer that cannot really be prayed by myself because my prayers are dependent upon the prayers of the others in the group. I am suggesting that dynamic corporate prayer has more to do with a group of people catching what is on God's heart than telling Him what is on their heart.

I did not grow up being exposed to this kind of prayer. In fact, I had been a pastor for many years before I had a chance to participate in this type of prayer experience at a Prayer Summit. That is not the only place this type of prayer can be experienced. As you will see, the components of dynamic corporate prayer can be integrated into a study class or fellowship group, applied to a family or large prayer meeting. They can be

> *I am advocating for a kind of prayer that is more dependent upon* listening *than it is* upon lists.

utilized in spontaneous praying or in a Sunday worship service. But this Prayer Summit is where I and many others were first exposed to it.

What was different about that time of prayer? I will answer this question by sharing what Phil Miglioratti, who has been involved in the Chicago Prayer Summit, wrote to help others catch this new approach.

Even for pastors and prayer leaders, the Prayer Summit is probably different than any meeting they have previously attended.

We worship, but this is not a praise and worship service. We read Scripture, but very differently than on a typical Sunday morning. We pray, but with a unique flow; this is not your Wednesday night prayer meeting. Nor is it merely a prayer retreat, designed for you to spend personal time with the Lord. Certainly not a Prayer Conference, do not expect any sermons, workshops, or study outlines.

The Prayer Summit utilizes all-of-the above but in such a unique way that it becomes wonderful to experience but difficult to describe.

Think of it as a place where all of God's children, red and yellow, black and white, can come together in a humility that produces Scriptural unity. It's an environment, which welcomes the expression of every person, culture and tradition. It's a prayer meeting where all have both the freedom to be themselves and the responsibility to serve others.

Our Facilitators: *Our facilitator is the Holy Spirit. He is the leader. He sets the agenda. A team of men and women are assigned to discern the voice of the Spirit as we journey in prayer together.*

Our Foundation: *Our foundation is the Word of God; it is our authority. Our prayers are both based upon and bound by the teaching and truths of Holy Scripture.*

Our Focus: *Our focus is Jesus Christ. We come to the Prayer Summit to seek Him, see Him, meet Him, hear Him, and obey Him.*

Our Format: *Our format is simple: psalms, hymns and spiritual songs. We gather in large groups, small groups, and individually.*

Our Freedom: *Since we have varied traditions, all are encouraged to be mindful of others, deferring, if necessary, for the sake of unity and harmony. At times, this means those who pray with exuberance may need to "tone it down." At other times, this* *may also mean those who are uncomfortable with the volume or emotional display need to give freedom and not take offense.*

The issue is not what is comfortable for or preferred from your experience. What matters is:

- *Has this been prompted and led by the Holy Spirit?*
- *Is it under the authority (in the name) of Christ?*
- *Does it bring glory (pleasure) to God?*
- *Is it contributing to what the Lord is doing in this meeting?*

While we all anticipate the blessing of personal time in the presence of Christ, the Prayer Summit is a rare opportunity for leaders to meet corporately with their Lord, like a staff meeting. It's like when Jesus walked and talked with His disciples.

Listen: to God, of course, but also to His voice expressed through others very different than yourself. So listen... To the Holy Spirit, To the facilitators, and To the prayers of one another.

Let your prayers be a result of our listening. Listen and you will be blessed by the fresh wind of the Holy Spirit and the body of Christ will receive a fresh word from our Lord and Leader.

Whatever you do, do unto the Lord...

Another way dynamic corporate prayer is different from most times of prayer is that it gives the group an opportunity to *do* Scripture rather than just *read* it. I remember a time when we were focusing on Jesus in worship and someone read from Revelation 5. In verse 12 it says the large crowd proclaimed its message with a *loud* voice. As the man read those verses, his voice remained the same volume but I sensed he wanted to shout it out! So, after he finished reading, I invited him to go back and re-read that portion of Scripture and to shout it out. He did and we did and it was a very appropriate time of powerful praise.

There have been times when a passage of Scripture is read about kneeling, so we have paused and invited people to kneel. Or to "take a position you would take if a king entered the room." Other times we have all raised our hands in praise or sat in silence. In our regular times of prayer, we don't normally take the opportunity to *do* just what the Scriptures say. As we take the time, it adds a more real and personal dimension to our prayers.

➢ **Blessed by Doing** – Look for an appropriate opportunity to *do* Scripture as you pray. When you are reading a passage of Scripture that mentions a specific action such as crying out, raising hands, standing, or being silent, don't just read it, do it.

1.2 How is it different from "individual prayer in a group setting?"

Dynamic corporate prayer should not be thought of as a replacement for any other style of praying. Its components are useful in contemplative prayer, spiritual warfare, intercession, and praise. In fact, the style of prayer I am advocating for in this book is not the only very powerful means of corporate prayer. Paul exhorts us to pray using "all kinds of prayers" (Eph 6:18). The kind of prayer that has flowed out of the Prayer Summit movement is not completely unique, but it is not as familiar as many other kinds of prayer.

If we grew up around prayer, then most of us grew up with what could be known as the "prayer microphone" type of corporate prayer. There may be 15 people in the room and Bill takes his opportunity to step up to the "prayer microphone" and pray what is on his heart. It is a good prayer. Then Mary takes her turn and prays through the requests that are closest to her. After her, Jane prays her burden. It is probable that most of

> *Dynamic corporate prayer should not be thought of as a replacement for any other style of praying.*

the 15 people pray and yet none of the prayers are connected to each other in any way. This is what I call "individual prayer in a group setting."

When I say dynamic corporate prayer I am referring to prayers that...

- are connected to what has just been prayed.
- hear and catch a prayer theme, and develop a flow.
- are influenced by the prayers of others and in turn influence the prayers of others.
- flow more from *listening* than from lists.
- focus on *agreement* or *harmonious* prayers.

➢ **Blessed by Doing** – The next time you are in a time of corporate prayer, pray prayers that are directly related to the previous prayer.

1.3 How is it different from intercessory prayer?

Generally speaking, intercession is prayer for one another or the needs around us that the Lord puts on our heart. Typically, there is a topic such as evangelism, a specific situation, or missions. It is prayer that comes in between the plans of the evil one and the person or people being prayed for. Its focus is nearly always horizontal. This is a wonderful and needed ministry. We need more people to enter into God's burden in this manner.

Dynamic corporate prayer, or summit-style prayer, also includes prayer for the needs of those around us and in our world, but that is not its starting point. Its focus is vertical. Its starting point is worship. The priority is the exaltation of God and the glory of His Son. I have learned that when we focus on God and His priorities, He will lead us to the specific ways He wants us to be praying for one another and for the needs around us.

1.4 What if we broadened the meaning of the question, "Would you lead us in prayer?"

I have the privilege of sharing at Western Seminary in Portland, Oregon a few times per year on the topic of dynamic corporate prayer. One day as I was concluding 4 hours of "show and tell" on the topic, I glanced at the clock and realized I had just about one minute to sum up all I wanted them to catch.

Here is what I said:

*I think I can say nearly everything I want you to walk away with in less than one minute. My hope is that because of our time together today the meaning of the question "Would you lead us in prayer?" has been enlarged. **From**: "Bill, would you lead us in prayer?" And Bill stands, speaks, we listen, he says amen, and he has led us in prayer. **To**: "Bill, would you lead us in prayer?" And Bill says, "Sure, I would be happy to lead us in prayer. I have been thinking about Psalm 90:14 (or a host of other verses or topics) which says, 'Satisfy us in the morning with Your unfailing love...' Let's close (or open) our time in prayer today by considering the things about God that deeply satisfy us. I will give you a moment to consider what you would like to say, then I will start, and let's have about 5 or 6 others of you follow right after me..." Then after Bill pauses for 10-15 seconds, he prays, "Father, Your grace deeply satisfies me." Then, someone else might say, "Father, the blood of Your Son deeply satisfied You and it deeply satisfies me." Or "Father, being part of Your Body has satisfied my deep need to belong." Perhaps others would mention, His peace, His mercy, His joy, or His calling, etc.*

The specifics of the illustration should change from setting to setting, but I think you get the picture. *Leading* a group in prayer can (and in most settings I would say *should*) include giving many people in the group an opportunity to meaningfully contribute to the prayer. It does not have to take any longer than if just one person prayed. Your leadership, your prayer direction, brings the opportunity for the group to pray in the power of unity.

When we ask someone to lead us in worship, we don't expect a solo, we expect him or her to do that which will help us express our hearts to the Lord. Why should it be different when we ask someone to lead us in prayer? Why not anticipate that the person who leads us in prayer would actually help us all pray rather than just pray on our behalf?

➤ **Blessed by Doing** – When you are in a group that will have a time of prayer, such as a Sunday School class, a home group, or a church leaders group, be prepared with a possible way you could help *facilitate*, rather than *lead* that prayer time. Then if called upon, facilitate the process.

When we ask someone to lead us in worship, we don't expect a solo, we expect him or her to do that which will help us express our hearts to the Lord.

1.5 Why do you use the word *facilitate* rather than *lead*? What is the difference between the two?

The specific role of the facilitator will be more fully addressed in Sections 6-8. But here is a brief answer.

I don't really expect that the meaning of the question, "Would you lead us in prayer?" (as mentioned in Question 1:4 above) will change any time soon. So, another way to describe the person who is responsible for the time of prayer is a *facilitator*. The hope is that they would not do the leading or the praying as much as they would provide encouragement and opportunities for others to do most of the praying. The most important thing is not how much or how well the facilitator may pray but rather how much and how well the others in the room pray. A good facilitator helps people get where God wants them to go, helps them connect with God and what He is doing. Sometimes they may be noticed, but they are not the center of attention.

On various occasions I have asked those who facilitate dynamic corporate prayer how they would describe the facilitation process. Here is a collection of their answers. They will further develop the distinction between facilitating prayer and leading a more traditional prayer meeting.

• Discerning where the Spirit of God is leading and how He is moving among us, and inviting others to enter in;

- Giving direction, focus and flow through the prayers we pray, the songs we sing, and the Scriptures we share, as well as through verbal instructions;
- Giving direction with a gentle, humble spirit, yet with a steady hand in constant dependence and trust in the Holy Spirit;
- Contributing toward a transforming encounter with God, His sovereignty and holiness;
- Noticing which door God is opening and inviting the participants to walk through it;
- Inviting the group to participate in a prayer activity the Lord has invited you to do.
- Modeling the role of a participant in everything we do or don't do, even our body language. How and when we participate or enter into the flow has influence, gives permission, suggests approval, and provides support or encouragement.

➤ **Blessed by Doing** – When you are in an extended time of prayer, consider how you might facilitate it. If you are responsible for the time of prayer, think through the bullet points above and let them shape your actions.

1.6 Do I really need to be involved in any kind of corporate prayer? Why can't I just pray by myself?

The short answer is "no." You don't need to be involved in corporate prayer. You can just pray by yourself. You also don't *need* to spend regular time in Scripture, or even spend time in prayer by yourself. But there are benefits from these disciplines you can only receive by engaging in them. So, perhaps a better question would be, "Will being involved in dynamic corporate prayer help me be more effective in my walk with Jesus and will it help me pray better prayers?" To this question, I can give a whole-hearted, "yes!"

The morning I wrote this section, I had some time with a good friend, Mike, who is moving out of our area. We reminisced about some good times together. He has walked with the Lord for many years. He mentioned that the first time he experience dynamic corporate prayer was at a retreat I was leading for our congregation. It helped his prayer experience be fuller. Years later, it still had an impact upon him.

It is not at all uncommon for pastors to mention to me at a Prayer Summit or in some other setting that the prayer they experienced there changed their lives.

I get to share regularly on the topic of corporate prayer in the classroom at Western Seminary in Portland, OR. After a time of about 45 minutes of this style of prayer a woman said to me, "I am going to graduate in about a month and this is the longest period of time I have ever prayed in a classroom setting." Unfortunately, many believers have not had the opportunity to experience the personal growth or the sense of His presence that comes from praying in this manner.

1.7 What is the value of dynamic corporate prayer? What difference does it make?

In addition to the other values referred to in other parts of this book, here are several things that happen in a time of corporate prayer that can't or don't happen in a personal time of prayer.

I can get to know God more as I hear people pray who have a different personality, background, or theological perspective. In Ephesians 1, Paul says that a reason why he is praying for the Ephesian saints is, "so that they would know Him better." This is a key reason to pray. In Colossians 2:2-3 there is a series of thoughts which shows how this can happen.

> *My purpose is that they may be encouraged in heart and united in love,* so that *they may have the full riches of complete understanding,* in order that *they may know the mystery of God, namely, Christ...* (my emphasis)

Paul's thinking begins with being united in love (prayer produces that kind of unity). This unity will lead them to the full riches of understanding. This will allow them to know the mystery of God, which is Jesus Christ.

On many occasions I have had my understanding of Jesus Christ enlarged and even corrected as I have heard the prayers of people who know Christ differently (and in many cases better) than I have known Him.

I can hear the heart of another believer better when I hear them speaking to their Father rather than when they are just speaking to me. In a safe environment, people speak more openly and deeply when they pray than when they speak to another.

> *On many occasions I have had my understanding of Jesus Christ enlarged and even corrected as I have heard the prayers of people who know Christ differently than I have known Him.*

One of the clear directives of Scripture is to pray for one another. Getting people into smaller groups (generally 4-6 people) and giving them the following instructions has produced some wonderful times of prayer.

- Randomly select the first person to pray – (based upon their birthday – "the person whose birthday is closest to today," their height – "beginning with the tallest person in your group," their first or last name – "alphabetically according to your first names," or some other means).

- Explain that this time of prayer is about your own personal needs, not the needs of others. ("Scripture says we are to pray for one another. This is an opportunity for you to share your personal needs and let others join you in that prayer.")

- Encourage them to consider, "the one thing you would most like the Lord to do in or for you personally." This helps people share more meaningful things rather than more distant things.

- Ask them to not share their prayer request with the others, but rather just to begin talking to their Father about their concern

Definitions

("As you begin, just climb up into the Father's lap and tell Him what is on your mind.")

- Instruct the others to listen carefully to the person praying so when it is time, they can join them and pray for their request.
- Let them know beforehand about how much time they will have for this time of prayer. Make sure that you give the group ample time to pray. It is not uncommon for this to take about 10 – 15 minutes per person. So a group of 6 people could easily pray in this setting for an hour or so.

As you pray in this manner you will see deeper relationship formed because of the deeper level of communication that has taken place.

It allows a group to worship together, listen together, make common requests, and rejoice together in His answers.

As we will see later, worship is a key component of dynamic corporate prayer. Personal worship is a needed discipline. So is corporate worship. I am not simply speaking of singing together. I am speaking about the sense of awe that a group can experience when they are together considering some aspect of God's great and wonderful nature.

I was with a few pastors in Northern Virginia. As we were praying, I sensed a transition was coming up. It seemed right for me to ask the group to get away for a period of time and just soak in their favorite "Jesus exalting passage of Scripture." When we returned, we had a wonderful time of worship simply by these brothers reading and praying from the freshness found in these passages.

It gives people an opportunity to ask and hear together. A pastor led a prayer retreat for the leadership of his congregation after being at a couple Pastors' Prayer Summits. At one point he sensed God had something He wanted to say to them as a group. So, he invited them to take an hour or so and simply ask God if there was anything He wanted to say to this team. When they returned, there were about a dozen people who shared something and all but one was on the topic of unity. Because this group asked together, they

33

heard together. It was a great confirmation to all of them that God had given them some very specific direction.

It enhances my own individual prayers because I can pray *off of* the prayers of others and they can do the same with mine. As we listen to the prayers of others, there are many times when one person's prayers spark a thought in another person. Because of the conversational nature of dynamic corporate prayer, it is not uncommon for several people to pray around one specific topic and even at times add to (or even complete) a thought someone else began. The way I understand this is that Jesus hears one prayer through many voices rather than many separate prayers.

In Matthew 18:19 Jesus uses an interesting word to describe agreement in prayer.

Again, I tell you that if two of you on earth agree about anything you ask for, it will be done for you by my Father in heaven.

The word translated, "agree" is the word from which the English language gets the word, "symphony." What a wonderful and creative illustration for corporate prayer. In a symphony many instruments play at the same time. But because they are all playing from the same score and under the same director, the music is complementary, not conflicting. As we listen to the Conductor and to the other instruments our contribution can enhance the overall time of prayer. Sometimes our prayers build upon the prayers of others, sometimes theirs builds upon ours. And sometimes your prayer is a confirmation to my prayer. This kind of prayer produces not only unity but also harmony. It is very hard to be a symphony all by yourself! Symphonic prayer can only be prayed with others. It is very hard to be a symphony all by yourself!

It allows me to agree with another prayer. Another important truth from Matthew 18:19 is the power of agreement. Saying "Amen" should be much more than the signal that my prayer is over or that what has just been prayed is one of my favorite topics. The word "Amen" is a means of communicating my receptivity to what I

34

have just heard. It is like swallowing a spiritual truth. It is stating that this is a prayer that I would have prayed if I had the words. It is adding the *weight* of my unspoken prayer to the prayer that has just been spoken. It is stating my agreement and therefore increasing our anticipation of God's answer. This is another unique aspect of corporate prayer.

> *It is very hard to be a symphony all by yourself!*

It makes good use of spiritual gifts. It is clear that whatever one's view of spiritual gifts may be, they seem to function best in a group setting. They are designed to build one another up. As we are praying with others in a group setting, we have opportunity to receive from the use of other people's gifts as well as express ours. Mercy is displayed through prayer. Teaching and learning happens as we pray. Wisdom is gleaned and encouragement takes place. And God performs healings and miracles. Corporate prayer allows us to benefit from, participate in, and appreciate God using people to impact others.

The transparency of one person in prayer can affect many others. I remember when Dave shared the phrase, "bold humility" with me. He was in a small country church when the Lord brought deep conviction to his heart. Without an altar call and even while the speaker was still speaking, he got up from his seat, went to the front of the church, laid face down at the altar and wept over his sin. He was completely unaware of how long he was there or what was going on around him. When he finally looked up, he saw that the preacher had stopped preaching and there were many other people who had followed his leadership. Many others got right with Jesus because of the "bold humility" of one person.

In extended times of prayer, it is very common for one person to share a deep need or conviction over sin and others respond. When one person leads out it gives not only permission but also encouragement for others to respond to the Lord.

These things take place because the orientation of corporate prayer is different than that of individual prayer. We are not thinking primarily about our requests. Instead we are joining with others to focus first on the Lord and secondly on the requests that flow from His heart.

> *When he finally looked up, he saw that the preacher had stopped preaching and there were many other people who had followed his leadership.*

So, does a person *need* to be involved in corporate prayer? No, but if they don't, there are many benefits they will miss out on which can cause them to grow more in their relationship with God as well as with others.

➢ **Blessed by Doing** – Review this list of the values of dynamic corporate prayer and look for an opportunity to share it with a prayer group. As you see other benefits of corporate prayer, add them to this list.

1.8 What commitments should the pray-ers make for dynamic corporate prayer to be most effective?

There are a few commitments that help make corporate prayer work well. As a group sees and accepts these, the Lord will be able to deepen the experience of the pray-ers.

A commitment to listen to the Lord and move in His direction, and at His pace. Just as each Hebrew that God led through the desert had the responsibility to keep an eye on the pillar of fire and the cloud, so also each person in a time of prayer has the responsibility to keep an ear tuned into the Lord and what He is doing. The fact that they are not the leader of the time of prayer does not release them from this responsibility. Times of corporate prayer work best to the degree that all of the participants are praying together under the direction of the Holy Spirit. The analogy of us being the Body of Christ is perhaps most evident in a prayer setting.

The hope is that each member of the Body will be in sync with the Head of the Body. They may not do or pray the same thing at the same time, but they are all aware of how the Lord is leading them as each one does his/her part.

A commitment to listen fully to the prayers of others – so we are not just hearing the words, but really catching the heart and spirit of what is being prayed. Typically we think if we are not saying the words, than we don't need to really engage in what is being said. The better each pray-er listens to the prayers of others, the better dynamic corporate prayer works.

A commitment to have my prayers relate to the prayers of other. Since I am not thinking about my prayer, but rather the prayer being prayed, I am available to hear how the Lord might want me to add to a certain topic of prayer.

A commitment to actively participate in the time of prayer. My level of comfort should not be the issue here. The issue is that I have an opportunity to be used by God, to add to the worship experience, to hear or observe what God is saying or doing, or to stand with my brother or sister at a specific point of need. If all (or even most) of the pray-ers actively participate in the process, the flow of God's mercy, grace, and wisdom can come through more channels.

Finally, *a commitment to the "ABC's" of corporate prayer* is necessary. I have heard Daniel Henderson describe these as Audible, Brief, and Clear. There may be times, even in a corporate setting, when it is appropriate for a prayer to be heard by only one or two people. But generally speaking, prayers that cannot be heard by the whole group hinder the value of corporate prayer. We should encourage the person praying to pray so the person on the other side of the room can hear them. Also, long prayers can kill meaningful times of corporate prayer. A good general rule is to encourage people to pray *single topic* prayers. Speeches or sermons in the form of a prayer are far more edifying for the one praying than the ones hearing! We should train people away from long, multi-topic prayers. Prayers that are clear and to the point, on the other hand, should be encouraged because of the impact they can have. For more on this topic see Question 2.2.

➤ **Blessed by Doing** – Pray a specific prayer about each of the five commitments above asking God to remind you of them. Then share them with a prayer group as you have opportunity.

1.9 Is this kind of prayer biblical? Do we see a biblical pattern for guided prayer experiences?

This is a good question. I know of nowhere in Scripture that specifically describes the kind of prayer referred to here as dynamic corporate prayer. Nor do I know of any place in Scripture that specifically describes the kind of preaching most preachers do, or the kind of worship that most churches are regularly engaged in. The same could be said of the kind or prayer most prayer meetings are modeled after, or our children's programs, or men's ministry times. But that doesn't mean it is wrong.

Here is what we do know. We know God wants us to pray together. The first thing Jesus teaches us about prayer in the Lord's Prayer is that there are times when we should pray together. The pronouns of the Lord's Prayer are plural. He says we should call him, *"Our* Father" and that we should ask Him to "give *us*… forgive *us*… lead *us*… and deliver *us*" (my em-phas-*us*). [1]

Many of the examples we have of prayer in the New Testament were prayers prayed with others. You see this in Acts 1:14, 2:42, 4:24, 6:4, 12:5&12, 13:2-3, 16:25, 20:36. You see it in the epistles in Colossians 4:2, 1 Timothy 2:1&8 and James 5:14. And in Revelation you see it in 4:11 and 5:9-14. And in Heaven you see the Cherubim and Seraphim are praying and worshiping together in Isaiah 6:1-3 and Revelation 4:8.

---

[1] Since the Lord's Prayer is the best model we have for prayer, I refer to it on several occasions in this book. For a fuller treatment on this, please see my gook, Living Prayer: The Lord's Prayer Alive in You. More information is available at www.livingprayer.net.

Definitions

We also know that worship was a key part of some of these times of prayer. In Acts 2, when the Holy Spirit came in a unique way, the apostles began speaking in other languages. Verse 11 tells us the content of those messages. They were "declaring the wonders of God..." In Acts 13, when leaders gathered for a time of worship, the Holy Spirit directed them to set aside Barnabas and Saul to be the first ordained missionaries of the early church. Public, corporate worship and prayer was a key ingredient in both the birth of the church on the day of Pentecost and the first New Testament missions movement.

Then in 1 Corinthians 14 we have the closest description of how the early church worshipped. According to verse 26 it was a highly participatory time. Whether or not one believes in the ongoing use of the specific spiritual gifts mentioned in this passage, we still get a clear glimpse of how the early church worshipped. Each person was part of the worship team. They came with their hearts and minds prepared to contribute to the overall process. There was prayer. There was music. There was instruction. There was edification. There was spontaneity. And there was order.

In 1 Corinthians 14 we have the closest description of how the early church worshipped. According to verse 26 it was a highly participatory time.

We also know that some of these times (and other times of prayer) were planned, at least to some degree. Acts 4:23 and following (specifically verse 24) provides us with an interesting example. These verses are the last verses in the story of the ruckus Peter and John caused by healing the lame man near the temple recorded in Acts 3. There was quite a backlash and they were arrested. Upon their release, the believers gathered and prayed. Verse 24 says, "When they heard this, they raised their voices *together* in prayer to God." The next seven verses records what they prayed.

Perhaps this is a generalization that Luke (the author) makes as he summarizes many individual prayers. Or perhaps one person prayed out loud and the others listened. But the text says that many people were speaking. So, perhaps this is an example of dynamic corporate prayer. None of us were there nor have we watched the video of what took place, but it certainly is a possibility that this prayer was prayed in a responsive manner. Perhaps Peter or John or some other leader said a phrase out loud and the rest of the people prayed that phrase back again. As I have been up front in different prayer settings, this kind of prayer has worked very well. Or this could be a composite prayer. It is possible that Peter prayed the first line or two, then John prayed, then some other leaders prayed.

Another example of dynamic corporate prayer could be seen in the Throne Room scene of Revelation 4 and 5. Again, we don't know why all these beings knew just what to say at the same time, but it certainly is a possibility that as the twenty-four elders fell before the throne and declared His worth in Revelation 4:9-11, many individuals were contributing different aspects of His worth.

As I have been in prayer settings and invited people to declare why Jesus is worthy, or what He is worthy to receive, many people contribute with words like what those elders said. What we want to remember is that when John first saw this happening, it was all very fresh to him and to those who were worshipping. Each word had deep meaning. Each phrase was shared from the heart of the elders.

Another interesting reality is on several occasions the Psalmist (generally King David) wrote out "A to Z" lists (of course it was in Hebrew, so it would be an "Aleph to Taw" list) when he wrote several Psalms. Psalm 25, 34, 37, 112, 119, and 145 are all acrostic Psalms. That means each verse begins with a consecutive letter of the Hebrew alphabet. So, as David was considering God, or as He was reveling in His law (Ps. 119) he wrote things out in such a way that they could be easily remembered. It is very doubtful that these Psalms were spontaneous. They required much thinking, and maybe some rewriting. They were probably written over a longer time span. Since most of the audience could not read at the time, this was a great way to help them pray or praise together.

Another Psalm, 136, is specifically designed to be read antiphonally. One person would declare a statement (the first half of each verse) and the people would respond to that statement with another prepared statement ("His love endures forever!"). Consider again the word picture in Matthew 18:19. Agreement in prayer is like the different instruments of a symphony each playing their part at the right time, following their own sheet of music under the direction of the Holy Spirit. *Symphonic* prayer – prayer from many people each contributing a harmonious part of the whole prayer – is another picture of what I am calling dynamic corporate prayer.

I would not fight over these specific examples, and I have no need to try to find exact examples of this type of prayer in Scripture, but I would say that Scripture certainly allows for and even leans toward creative, dynamic, corporate prayer that is in some way planned, guided, or orchestrated.

➢ **Blessed by Doing** – Look for more Biblical examples of dynamic corporate prayer and add to this list.

United and Ignited

2. Components – What are the components of dynamic corporate prayer?

Good preaching experiences rarely just happen. Nor do delightful times of worship. Sometimes a very experienced preacher or worship leader is asked to preach or lead worship spontaneously and God uses it in a powerful way. Or sometimes God interrupts the preacher or worship leader's plan and makes His specific will known to them "on the spot." They go with it and it ends up much better than anyone could have planned. These are delightful times, but more the exception rather than the rule. And a key reason why the Lord was able to use these people in a setting like that is because of the many hours they spent in doing the seemingly mundane things so that when the opportunity presented itself, they were prepared to do the spontaneous things.

Though dynamic corporate prayer should not be as predictable as the typical sermon or time of worship, there still needs to be much preparation involved. There are some important components that typically go into meaningful times of corporate prayer.

The most important factor in dynamic corporate prayer is the movement of God in that specific setting. When His presence is evident, when His voice is clear, when His will is being accomplished, when it is obvious that people are encountering Him, we are able to come away from that time with a clear sense that it was a meaningful time of prayer. So, clearly, the most important factor in dynamic corporate prayer is the activity of God in the process.

And there are several other factors God uses to get us to that place. These are developed in Questions 2.1 – 2.4 below.

➢ **Blessed by Doing** – The next time you have responsibility for a time of prayer (with your family or with a group from church or work) go to it having thought and prayed about it.

2.1 Does the facilitator really make that much difference in the quality of the prayer time?

I am convinced that the most important *human* factor in dynamic corporate prayer is the facilitator and his/her ability to cooperate with the Lord so that people really are able to connect with God. I have come away from some times of corporate prayer with a clear sense that there was no facilitation at all, or that the facilitator really did not help the people pray most effectively. And sometimes, I have been the one facilitating!

We will say more about the specific role of the facilitator later, but at this point I just want to stress the significance of that role. I remember seeing the tear-drops fall from Dr. Joe's face and wet the floor in front of his chair as he poured out his heart to God about His glory and goodness and how he longed for each person to know the love and forgiveness of the Savior. I remember him sharing his personal struggles, confessing his own sin. His transparency not only instructed us but also encouraged us to be transparent. We cannot lead people where we have not been or where we are not going.

> *I am convinced that the most important human factor in dynamic corporate prayer is the facilitator...*

My own experience has convinced me that I facilitate best when I don't forget that I am facilitating, but at the same time remember to be become a participant. This cannot be simply about helping *those people* meet with God. It has to be about us entering in as well.

➢ **Blessed by Doing** – The next time you are praying with a group, consider what the facilitator did or did not do to assist the prayer time. Do this even if you are the facilitator.

2.2 What role do the *pray-ers* have in a quality time of dynamic corporate prayer?

The second most important human factor that determines the quality of dynamic corporate prayer is the desire of those in the room. If there is a great desire for them to encounter God, chances are very good they will. If there is something else on their heart or mind than pressing into the Lord, or if they have been told they must be there when they don't want to be, then... well, good luck.

I want to be very clear here. I am not referring to the level of spiritual maturity, or Bible knowledge, or ministry experience. Brand new believers can enter into meaningful times of prayer as well as (and maybe even better than) believers who have walked with the Lord for many years. Length of time with Jesus is not the factor. Neither is age, gender, appearance, occupation, theological perspective, or denominational preference. The key factor is a heart that is not only willing but desirous to draw closer to the Living God. It was Mary's heart (in Luke 10, John 11, and John 12) that caused her to regularly be at Jesus' feet. In 1 Corinthians 14:26, each participant came ready to participate.

The best times of prayer are when the pray-ers are ready to pray with a surrendered heart and a whole heart. A surrendered heart does not hold on. And a whole heart does not hold back. A surrendered heart says, "Not my will be done." A whole heart says, "All I am is Yours."

It is not about convincing people that this is what they need. It is about discovering the people God has already convinced. He is a much better convincer than we are. When God convinces them (and He can do that in many different ways)

> *The key factor is a heart that is not only willing but desirous to draw closer to the Living God.*

then the facilitation process is a real joy. And when there are people there who don't want to move closer to the Lord, they don't want to enter in, it not only makes it more difficult for the facilitator, but it really can keep the whole group from going where Jesus wants to take it.

Even though we do want as many people as possible to experience the Lord through dynamic corporate prayer, we want to make sure that the core of the group is there because they are thirsty for more of Him. When people come thirsty, it is not a difficult process to help them drink from the Living Water. So, as you invite people to a time of prayer, be clear about what the purpose of the time is. Let them know that it is about deepening their relationship with the Lord. That it is about finding out what is on His heart and pursuing it. Don't "bait and switch." If you do, the switch may end up being used on you. For more on this, see Question 1.8 above.

➤ **Blessed by Doing** – Consider a recent time of prayer. To what degree were the pray-ers engaged? What assisted or hindered them?

2.3 What role does our theology of prayer play in dynamic corporate prayer?

What we believe about prayer is another significant component in a meaningful time of prayer. This is not the place and I am not sure I am the person to write a complete theology of prayer. But I can and do want to share a perspective on prayer that, when adopted, will make your prayer times more dynamic. Let me offer you this perspective as we think about our understanding and belief about prayer.

All theological camps agree that prayer is a vital discipline in our walk with Jesus. They agree that Scripture gives us clear commands to pray. They agree that Scripture tells us that our prayers matter – that God answers prayers. They agree that prayer is a primary way we come into deeper relationship with God. And they agree that the

Bible is the best source of our prayers. It is a beautiful picture of the Body of Christ when those who emphasize God's sovereignty and those who emphasize man's responsibility can pray in harmony because of their points of agreement.

There are at least these three factors or aspects to prayer. Or, we could say there are three reasons to pray. The first is the *obedience* factor. Jesus did not say "If you pray," He said "When you pray" (Luke 11:2[2]). He told parables to His disciples "to show them that they should always pray and not give up" (Luke 18:1). Paul told the Romans to be "faithful in prayer" (Romans 12:12[3]); the Colossians to "devote" themselves to prayer (Colossians 4:2[4]); and the Thessalonians that they should "Pray continually" (1 Thessalonians 5:17). On several occasions Paul asked people to pray for him (Ephesians 6:19[5], Colossians 4:3[6], 2 Thessalonians 3:1[7], Hebrews 13:18[8]).

> *It is a beautiful picture of the Body of Christ when those who emphasize God's sovereignty and those who emphasize man's responsibility can pray in harmony because of their points of agreement.*

If for no other reason, we should pray because God has told us to. He is God, we are not. He calls the shots, we bow in humble and grateful obedience. In one sense, that really is and should be reason enough. If we never saw any results from prayer, if none of our prayers were ever answered, it would still be right for us to pray simply because our Maker and

[2] Luke 11:2b He said to them, "When you pray, say..."
[3] Romans 12:12 Be joyful in hope, patient in affliction, faithful in prayer.
[4] Colossians 4:2 Devote yourselves to prayer, being watchful and thankful.
[5] Ephesians 6:19 Pray also for me, that whenever I open my mouth, words may be given me so that I will fearlessly make known the mystery of the gospel,
[6] Colossians 4:3 And pray for us, too, that God may open a door for our message, so that we may proclaim the mystery of Christ, for which I am in chains
[7] 2 Thessalonians 3:1 Finally, brothers, pray for us that the message of the Lord may spread rapidly and be honored, just as it was with you.
[8] Hebrews 13:18 Pray for us. We are sure that we have a clear conscience and desire to live honorably in every way.

Master has told us to. But there are reasons why He has told us to pray.

The second factor is the *functional* factor. When we pray, things happen differently than when we do not pray. Prayer matters. God answers prayer. When most of us think of prayer, this is what we think about. We know enough stories, and we have enough personal stories, of situations that turned out differently because we or someone else took a request before God's throne.

God's plan is not only to get us to heaven, but also to get heaven to us and through us to the world around us. And He wants to use us in the process. Part of the Lord's Prayer tells us to pray "... on earth as it is in heaven" (Matthew 6:10). There is way too much on earth that does not reflect heaven. And there is way too much heaven that earth knows nothing about. Prayer is a key part of the process and plan of God to correct that. As we pray, more of heaven comes to earth. His name is revealed and revered. His kingdom is established and expanded. His will is known and done. The bumper sticker cliché really is true; "Prayer changes things." And as we pray we find changes taking place not only around us but also in us. As I pray, more of heaven gets into me. More of the life and character of Jesus comes to me as I spend time in His presence. So, one of the first *things* it changes is me.

But there is another factor to prayer that is not as well known. This third factor is the *relational* factor. In its essence, prayer is not a formula, it is a conversation. It is communication between the created and the Creator. Think of it! We can actually have an exchange of thoughts and ideas that results in two beings (one with a capitol "B" and one with a lowercase "b") having more things in common. Amazing! Prayer is essentially a relational exchange.

God is very serious about developing a relationship with us. He created us for this purpose. When mankind rebelled and turned away from Him, He called out for us to turn back (Genesis 3:8[9]).

---

[9] Genesis 3:18 Then the man and his wife heard the sound of the LORD God as he was walking in the garden in the cool of the day, and they hid from the LORD God among the trees of the garden.

48

Components

When we did not turn back, He came to us (John 1:14[10]). When we did not receive Him, it just killed Him (2 Corinthians 5:15[11])! The Father is so serious about having a relationship with us that He wrote a whole book about it. Jesus is so serious about it that He set aside everything, including unbroken, eternal, fellowship with His Father and His own plans, glory, comfort, dignity and life to make it happen (Philippians 2:6[12], John 17:5[13]). The Holy Spirit is so serious about it that He has come to reside in each follower of Jesus to make sure that what got started would be brought to completion (Ephesians 1:13-14[14], Philippians 1:6[15]). God's deep desire to have a relationship with us is the crux and the context of the cross. There is no greater theme than God's commitment to have a relationship with us.

> *When we did not turn back, He came to us. When we did not receive Him, it just killed Him!*

Relationships do not happen without communication. The highest purpose of our communication with God – our times of prayer – is to develop a deeper love relationship with our God.

So why should we pray? 1) Because God has told us to. 2) Because God answers prayer. 3) Because through prayer we get to develop a deeper relationship with our Creator and Redeemer!

The cool thing is that as we focus on the third factor, we

[10] John 1:14 The Word became flesh and made his dwelling among us. We have seen his glory, the glory of the One and Only, who came from the Father, full of grace and truth.
[11] 2 Corinthians 5:15 And he died for all, that those who live should no longer live for themselves but for him who died for them and was raised again.
[12] Philippians 2:6 Who, being in very nature God, did not consider equality with God something to be grasped,
[13] John 17:5 And now, Father, glorify me in your presence with the glory I had with you before the world began.
[14] Ephesians 1:13-14 And you also were included in Christ when you heard the word of truth, the gospel of your salvation. Having believed, you were marked in him with a seal, the promised Holy Spirit, 14who is a deposit guaranteeing our inheritance until the redemption of those who are God's possession—to the praise of his glory.
[15] Philippians 1:6 being confident of this, that he who began a good work in you will carry it on to completion until the day of Christ Jesus.

automatically fulfill the first two factors. As we focus on the relational aspect of prayer, we fulfill the commands to pray and we see answers to prayer. The sad thing is that if we focus on either of the first two factors, we may miss the primary reason for prayer; a deeper relationship.

➢ **Blessed by Doing** – The next time you pray with others, notice if any prayers specifically focus on relationship (the third point above.) Pray at least one prayer that is focused solely on relationship with the Lord.

2.4 What are the functional components of dynamic corporate prayer?

In addition to the role of the facilitator, the participants, and our theology of prayer, there are four other specific components that are necessary for dynamic corporate prayer. In fact, in my mind, the "full name" for the kind of prayer I am advocating would be *Spirit-led, Worship-fed, Scripture-based, corporate prayer.* Or, as someone who recently heard me explain these said, "Sprit-led, Worship-fed, Scripturally-read, Corporately-said." Maybe a bit too much rhyming here!

These four items – prayer that is led by His Spirit more than our agendas – prayer that is fed and fueled by worship more than our requests – prayer that is based on and flows from Scripture more than our thoughts – and prayer that encourages all the people to participate in a natural flow – *these are the key components of meaningful, creative, dynamic corporate prayer.* It is dynamic prayer because it is Spirit-led, worship-fed, and Scripture-based. It is corporate prayer because it is more than individuals praying unrelated prayers.

The idea of *corporate* prayer has been and will continue to be addressed throughout this book. The next three Sections of questions will focus on the role of the *Holy Spirit*, the role of *worship*, and the role of the *Scriptures* in dynamic corporate prayer.

3. The Holy Spirit – What is the role of the Holy Spirit in dynamic corporate prayer?

At that first Prayer Summit I referenced earlier, I remember hearing Dr. Joe say something like, "We are not sure what we are doing here. We have done this a few times now, but that doesn't make us experts. We are trusting the Holy Spirit to guide us as we go along. If we catch what He is doing we will all be changed. If we don't catch it, well, we've had a nice time at the beach."

Trusting in the Holy Spirit to lead a time of dynamic corporate prayer is the most important thing a facilitator can do. But, let me make it clear that I do not mean we should take an *anything goes* attitude. Being led by the Spirit of God *encourages*, not discourages, orderliness, careful and prayerful planning, and the use of wisdom, boldness, and restraint. But it also means that we do not come to a time of prayer locked into how each moment will be used, how each prayer will be prayed, or how each person will participate. We need to be open to His surprises. Often He will override our prayerful planning with something far better; something we never imagined. We could say we are engaged in *planned spontaneity*. We come with a deep desire to spend time with Him and a confidence that as we draw near to Him, He will draw near to us as well.

As I have had the opportunity to facilitate in a city that has had multiple, annual Prayer Summits, I often ask the question, "Who here has been to this Prayer Summit before?" Typically, more than half of the hands go up. Then I restate the question emphasizing the word, *this* Prayer Summit – meaning the one we are presently attending. The obvious answer is that none of us have been to *this*

Prayer Summit before. The point is that if we view this time of dynamic corporate prayer as something that will be just like the last time of dynamic corporate prayer, we will tend to function on our own experience or thoughts and miss the beautiful place the Holy Spirit wants to take us.

> *Often He will override our prayerful planning with something far better; something we never imagined.*

As we consider this crucial part of facilitating, we should start with a confidence that the Holy Spirit wants to lead us, which is the topic of the next question.

➢ **Blessed by Doing** – Avoid all prayer *ruts*. Anticipate the Holy Spirit to bring freshness to your next time of corporate prayer.

3.1 How can I be sure the Holy Spirit will lead us in dynamic corporate prayer?

Please consider one of the *craziest* statements Jesus ever made. He is with His disciples the night before He will be crucified. It is what we call the Upper Room Discourse of John 13-17. In John 16:7 He says, "But I tell you the truth: It is for your good that I am going away. Unless I go away, the Counselor will not come to you; but if I go, I will send Him to you."

If the disciples were at all drowsy that night, I am sure this statement woke them right up. "What? We have spent three years with this man and we are now convinced he really is God in human flesh, and He is now telling us that it is good for us that He leaves! How can that be?" Is it really better to have the Spirit of God *in* us than to have the Son of God *with* us? That is clearly what Jesus taught.

Obviously, Jesus knew what He was talking about. It really is better to be a temple of the Holy Spirit, in which the God-head in the form of His Spirit dwells in us, than to be simply a witness to what Jesus did when He was on earth. The key difference is that now Jesus is not only with us everywhere we go, but is *in* us and can direct us from our innermost being.

Based upon this truth, the Scriptures tell us that it is right for us to develop a conviction that the Holy Spirit will guide us. Consider the following verses and thoughts.

The key to what is known as the "Good Shepherd" chapter – John 10 – seems to revolve around the fact that Jesus and His sheep can and do hear each other's voices. Notice especially verses 3, 5, 16, and 27. Jesus is still the Good Shepherd and He still wants us, through His Holy Spirit, to "hear His voice."

Romans 8:14 says, "...because those who are led by the Spirit of God are the sons of God." One of the evidences of being a true child of God, of receiving eternal life from Him, is that we now follow the leadership of the Spirit of God.

In Galatians 5, capping off a key passage on living by the Spirit rather than by our own sinful desires, Paul instructs us that, "Since we live by the Spirit, let us also keep in step with the Spirit" (v. 25). Again, based upon the life we have received from the Holy Spirit, we are now invited to live that out by keeping pace with Him. The Holy Spirit is committed to helping us keep in step with what He is doing and saying.

The most often repeated phrase of the New Testament is always stated by Jesus. Seven times in the Gospels and seven times in the book of Revelation Jesus says, "He who has an ear to hear, let Him hear..." Jesus wants us, as His followers, to hear what He is saying.

We are living in a culture today that thinks it is weird and even dangerous to think that a person can actually hear God's voice. And I am very aware of the abuses that have taken place under the guise of, "hearing God's voice." But this is a case when we dare not throw the baby out with the bath water! We can enter into a serious error on this topic if we move too far either one way or the other. We dare not think that God is silent today, and we dare not think that every thought we have is the result of something He has said to us. We must walk in a careful, prayerful balance.

But Scripture gives clear indication that we can be confident that as we live our lives and as we seek to lead others in prayer, the Holy Spirit not only is "out there somewhere" but that He is dwelling inside of us and wants to lead us in the process.

Blessed by Doing – Tell the Lord you really do trust the Holy Spirit and will seek to be sensitive to His leadership, especially as you facilitate prayer.

3.2 How can I be sure I will hear His voice?

Now that's a different question!

I can be confident that Jesus, through the Holy Spirit, wants to lead us. I can't be as confident that you or I will recognize His voice and respond to it. It has been my prayer for years and years that I would be more sensitive to His Spirit. That I would recognize the voice of the Shepherd and respond well to it every time He speaks. I don't know where you are in this process. I know that even though I have such a long way to go, I am better at this now than I was years ago. For me, this is an ongoing prayer and process.

A verse I have often prayed is the last portion of John 15:5. There Jesus makes it very clear, "Apart from me you can do nothing." Here is what I have come to believe about this verse. It is not that I can do *nothing* apart from Jesus. I *can* do all kinds of things apart from him. That is precisely the problem! I have preached enough to be able to preach without Him. I have facilitated prayer enough to be able to facilitate without Him. But when I do things apart from Him, it really does add up to *nothing*! I don't want to live or especially facilitate corporate prayer apart from Him.

> *It is not that I can do nothing apart from Jesus. I can do all kinds of things apart from him. That is precisely the problem!*

Another verse applies this directly to prayer. Romans 8:26 says that the Spirit of God not only helps us because we are weak in the area of prayer, but also that we don't even know how or what to pray. We are so helpless that we can't even ask for help without the help of the Holy Spirit! But that does not leave us hopeless. When we cooperate with the Holy Spirit, He will provide the help we need. He will speak in ways we can hear and understand. He will guide us in our prayer. He is very willing to lead us.

So, will we hear His voice? Will we follow His leadership if and when we hear it? I think the most honest answer to this question is, "Yes, we will seek to. Therefore, we will try to be completely dependent on Him. And when we hear Him, we will do our best to respond to what He says."

Blessed by Doing – Pray a prayer from the two verses above (John 5:15 and Romans 8:26) stating your complete dependence upon the Lord and relate it directly to when you pray and/or facilitate prayer.

3.3 How can I deal with distractions to hearing His Voice?

"But there are so many distractions to hearing His voice!" You are right about that. In fact, sometimes I am too distracted to know all of what distracts me! But I can identify some of them. The ones I am most familiar with are…
- my own sense of responsibility to make sure something is happening
- the desires and expectations of others (spoken or just assumed)
- the way we did things the last time
- a general dullness of my spirit
  So, to overcome these distractions, my responsibility is…
- to see that my first responsibility is to keep in step with Him
- to make His desires most prominent in my life
- to not let the past be my standard for the present
- to keep my spirit fresh in Him

But now, let me share with you some very good news. Even though, as a facilitator, I must seek to hear God's voice in the process, the accomplishment of His desires during a time of prayer are not limited to my ability to hear Him at any given moment! Much of the time the role of the facilitator is to simply recognize that what just happened or is happening is exactly what He wants to happen. Sometimes it is to recognize things He doesn't want to have happen. But much of the time, I catch up with what He is doing rather than know about it beforehand.

So, I have developed a conviction. I want to listen for and to the Holy Spirit on all occasions. On those occasions when He speaks and I hear Him clearly, I will act. On those occasions when He doesn't seem to be speaking or I don't seem to be hearing, I will watch and wait, and see if I can notice what He may be saying or doing. During those times I have found it is always safe to "turn our eyes upon Jesus," worship Him, and *fix* them there for awhile.

On those occasions when He speaks and I hear Him clearly, I will act.

Blessed by Doing – Reread the last paragraph above and turn it into a prayer. Then, when you facilitate prayer in the future, restate this to the group in some way.

3.4 How does He lead us?

Since we know that we need His leadership and that He wants to provide leadership, the most important question becomes, how does He lead us?

First of all, God can communicate to whomever He wants, whenever He wants, in any way He wants. He doesn't need to follow my pattern or any other pattern. That being said, I have found there are a few general principles He seems to normally follow.

• He will not lead us to do anything contrary to the clear teaching of His Word. If He said it then, He still means it.

- He will not lead us to do anything contrary to His nature.
- He will lead those who...
  - want to do His will (John 7:17[16])
  - are humble (Psalm 25:9[17])
  - fear Him (Psalm 25:12, 14[18])
  - trust Him (Proverbs 3:5-6[19])
  - serve Him and want to hear Him (1 Samuel 3:10[20])
  - seek Him (Matthew 7:7[21])
  - have a pure heart (Matthew 5:8[22])
- He will often times lead us with confirmation, repeating the message through various means. (2 Corinthians 13:1[23])

These are true and accurate principles that are helpful to know and follow, but they may not help much in the moment when you are facilitating prayer. So you may be asking, "How is He going to lead me?" Actually, I can't tell you how He will lead you, but I can tell you how He has led other people, and how He has led me in specific settings of prayer. Here are a few ways.

A *highlight* from a song or Scripture – when I hear Scripture read or a song sung, I simply try to *listen* to the words. It is interesting how over-familiarity will hinder our ability to hear something fresh. Many times as I am listening, the Lord seems to highlight a word or

---

[16] John 7:17 If anyone chooses to do God's will, he will find out whether my teaching comes from God or whether I speak on my own.

[17] Psalm 25:9 He guides the humble in what is right and teaches them his way.

[18] Psalm 25:12 Who, then, is the man that fears the LORD? He will instruct him in the way chosen for him. 14 Who, then, is the man that fears the LORD? He will instruct him in the way chosen for him.

[19] Proverbs 3:5-6 Trust in the LORD with all your heart and lean not on your own understanding; in all your ways acknowledge him, and he will make your paths straight.

[20] 1 Samuel 3:10 The LORD came and stood there, calling as at the other times, "Samuel! Samuel!" Then Samuel said, "Speak, for your servant is listening."

[21] Matthew 7:7 Ask and it will be given to you; seek and you will find; knock and the door will be opened to you.

[22] Matthew 5:8 Blessed are the pure in heart, for they will see God.

[23] 2 Corinthians 13:1 This will be my third visit to you. "Every matter must be established by the testimony of two or three witnesses."

phrase. It is like those words are bigger or heavier, or like an accented syllable in a word. I notice them more. When this happens, I try to listen more carefully. Most of the time this is God getting my attention. Often times I will simply ask the Lord at that moment how He wants us to pray from this truth. Once I ask that question the answer often seems to be quite clear.

A very *crisp thought* that fits the situation – I have many thoughts going through my mind during a time of prayer. But every now and then there is a very clear, crisp thought that is, frankly, a better thought for that situation than I am used to thinking. A pastor friend of mine says. "It sounds like me, but it is not what I would think." When this happens, I try to pay more close attention.

A *picture* of what may happen – As someone is praying, I may see, in my mind's eye, a certain person moving over to stand next to them to pray with them. So, at the right time, I will ask that person to do what I saw happen. Or as I have heard someone reading a section of Scripture, I may have a picture of the group responding in a certain way. For example to read the section phrase by phrase and let us repeat the words after them. So, when the person completes the passage – or even as they begin to read the passage – I have asked them to begin again and allow us to do what I saw.

A *distant sense* or thought that grows – Sometimes there is a very small thought that continues to expand and come closer to the front of my mind. It is like the cloud Elijah's servant saw coming toward Mt. Carmel. As it gets closer, I begin to recognize that the Holy Spirit might want to use that thought in some way.

A *reoccurring thought* that eventually fits the situation – Similar to the *distant* thought mentioned above, sometimes there is a thought that reoccurs several times during a time of prayer. At first I might not think it is very significant, but after it comes back a few times, I begin to think it may be more than just my thought.

Confirmation *through others* – There may be a normal thought I have and just as I am thinking about it, someone else prays a very similar thought. Or someone may read a verse that reflects the same idea. Or someone may sing a song on the same topic. I have been in several settings when someone began to read a Scripture that was the very verse(s) I had my eyes on in my Bible. And there have been times when two people have begun to sing exactly the same song in exactly the same key at exactly the same time. This is another indication that it is more than coincidence.

When someone reads or prays there is an *extra clarity and conviction* that comes with it – Another way I have sensed the leading of the Holy Spirit is when someone prays or reads a verse it is just *different*. There is almost a prophetic sense to it. It seems weightier or louder (though not in the sense of more decibels) or more clear or anointed. Often times when this happens, the Holy Spirit wants us to pay more attention to what has been said or read. I want to emphasize here that most of the time when this happens, the one speaking is not necessarily trying to make anything happen. They may be completely unaware of the weight of what they are saying. The difference is not so much in the saying as in the hearing.

Receiving His leadership should not be seen as either mechanical or magical. On one hand, we should not rely on any specific steps or formula. God doesn't fit well into formulas. On the other hand, we should not think of hearing the Lord as some kind of magical activity. He uses His word, our minds, those around us, and many other sources to draw our attention to His messages to us.

Just as when I call my wife on the phone, I don't say, "Marilyn, hello, this is Dennis calling," so also may we each get to a point where we will be able to hear and recognize the direction of the Holy Spirit as we lead others in prayer.

> *Receiving His leadership should not be seen as either mechanical or magical.*

➤ **Blessed by Doing** – Which of the seven ways mentioned above has the Holy Spirit led you? Tell Him you want to be open to any and all ways He may lead you as you facilitate prayer and ask Him to make you very sensitive to His leading.

United and Ignited

4. Worship – What is the role of worship in dynamic corporate prayer?

Soon after Prayer Summits first began, Dr. Joe defined them as, *A prolonged, typically four-day, life changing worship experience attended by a diversity of Christian leaders from a specific, geographic community whose sole purpose is to seek God, His kingdom, and His righteousness with an expectation that God will create and guide them through a humbling, healing, uniting process, which will lead them to a unity of heart, mind and mission and qualify them for the blessing of God.*

A very interesting thing about this definition is that it does not contain the word "prayer." He described a Prayer Summit as a *worship* experience. From the beginning worship has been a key component of Prayer Summits. In fact, a major goal of Prayer Summits and other times of dynamic corporate prayer should be to get people to appreciate more and stand more in awe of our wonderful, holy, triune God.

The desired end result of a Prayer Summit (or any other season of prayer) is that a community would be *impacted* by the presence of God through His church. But the process behind a Prayer Summit is to help people see that the church will never impact their community unless they themselves are a *healthy* community. And we will never be a healthy community unless we walk in *unity*. We will never walk in unity unless we walk in genuine *humility*. And we will never come to the place of genuine humility unless we linger in *worship* around the throne of a holy God. So, throughout a Prayer Summit, we are always looking for the way(s) the Holy Spirit wants to increase our awareness of His holiness. Once we are there we at least have the opportunity of walking in humility, unity, and health so we can impact our community.

> **Blessed by Doing** – In your last time of corporate prayer, what role did worship have? Why or why not? How could it have a more prominent role next time?

4.1 What role do songs play in facilitating dynamic corporate prayer?

Simply put, songs are vital to most times of dynamic corporate prayer. It is not uncommon in a Prayer Summit setting to sing dozens of songs each day. These songs don't come from a predetermined list, but rather from the minds and hearts of the participants. One song leads to another. When the second song is complete, a third song takes us further than the previous one did. Sometimes prayers and Scriptures are mixed together with them in a well orchestrated worship experience. But we are not the one who designed it. It was designed by the Holy Spirit and produced by the participants.

Beginning a time of prayer with a song gathers people together, but its purpose should be far more than that. It should also point people in a specific direction.

One time after beginning a session singing "On Christ the Solid Rock I Stand" I made the observation that we were honoring Jesus as the Solid Rock and asked a question that allowed us to worship well. I simply asked, "What else is He? Let's declare other names or descriptions of Jesus by saying, 'On Christ the _____ (you fill it in) I stand.'" For several minutes people declared, "On Christ the Lamb of God I stand. On Christ the Word of God I stand. On Christ the Alpha and Omega I stand. On Christ the way, the truth, and the life I stand." These declarations flowed from the fact that we just sang about Jesus. These words gave us an opportunity to not only get a good start to the time of prayer, but they allowed us to get a Jesus-focused start to it.

There are reasons why two New Testament Scriptures encourage the saints to sing together (Ephesians 5:19[24] and Colossians 3:16[25]). According to these verses, as we sing with both our voices and our hearts we are expressing an evidence of the work of the Holy Spirit in our midst, we are teaching one another by speaking truth together, and we are forming a choir that is singing to "an Audience of One," expressing

Beginning a time of prayer with a song gathers people together, but its purpose should be far more than that. It should also point people in a specific direction.

corporate gratitude to Him. Singing together allows our spirits to mingle around a specific truth. It unites us as few other activities can do.

When we see the worship service around the throne in Heaven portrayed in Revelation 4 and 5, songs are a key part of what we will be doing. Singing allows us to express our hearts in deeper ways then words. It releases something from our souls and spirits that is added to what our minds are processing. This allows us to encounter God with more of our entire being. And when we do this with other whole-hearted worshipers, the end result is exponentially greater than if we were alone.

As we facilitate a time of prayer, a song or a series of songs can set a clear direction for prayer. If, for example, we are preparing to receive communion, we may want to encourage people to sing songs that express God's love for us or songs that specifically mention the cross. They can also reinforce what has just been prayed or read. If someone reads Ephesians 2 about God's wonderful grace, singing John Newton's *Amazing Grace* or Chris Tomlin's newer version or

---

[24] Ephesians 5:19 Speak to one another with psalms, hymns and spiritual songs. Sing and make music in your heart to the Lord...

[25] Colossians 3:16 Let the word of Christ dwell in you richly as you teach and admonish one another with all wisdom, and as you sing psalms, hymns and spiritual songs with gratitude in your hearts to God.

some other song about grace gives us time to reflect on that theme.

I was scheduled to preach in a congregation so they also asked me to facilitate a time of prayer for their combined adult Sunday School class between two services. As I prayed about the time, I kept thinking about a certain hymn. Honestly, I can't recall which one it was, but it contained much good, Biblical truth, so to begin the time of prayer, I did not say, "Let's open our Bibles." I said, "Let's open in our hymnals." And we used the verses of that song as an outline for a very good time of prayer.

A song is also a great way to help get us back on track if we have wandered. If we are praying about His holiness and someone begins praying about their missionary friends in South America, singing one of the many songs about holiness can be a gentle reminder of the theme we had not yet completed.

➤ **Blessed by Doing** – Include a song in the next time of corporate prayer you facilitate and ask the people to pray prayers directly related to it as in one of the example above.

4.2 Can we worship without songs? If so, how?

Singing is a wonderful way to express corporate or individual worship, but it is not the only way. Since the essence of worship is recognizing and expressing God's *worth*, there are many different expressions of worship that can make our times of prayer more dynamic.

I was asked to facilitate a couple hours of prayer for a congregation on a Saturday morning. To start the second hour I divided the large group into 5 smaller groups. I assigned each group one of the first 5 chapters of book of Revelation, reminding them that the full title of that book is not the "Revelation of Charts" but the "Revelation of Jesus Christ." I encouraged them to find out as much as they could about Jesus from their chapter. After a few minutes I invited them to come in silence, pick up a colored marker and write a word or short phrase on pieces of butcher paper that were on the walls. The words, "Jesus, You are..." were written near the top of the pages. They were to write only one word or phrase at a time, but they could come as many times as they wanted. I also asked them not to worry if someone else wrote *their* word or phrase. Just write it again.

As the words went up on the paper we began to see more and more of Jesus. After several minutes of writing, I invited the entire group to gather around the pages and speak to Jesus using someone else's words on the paper. For 15 to 20 minutes we had a very glorious worship service even though there was no singing.

Several years ago I was facilitating a Pastors Prayer Summit on the Oregon Coast. The nearly 20 pastors in the circle were enjoying a meaningful time of praise. During this time, the thought came to me that we should take some time individually and "write a psalm." As I pondered the idea, it seemed a bit risky to me, but I had a peace that this was our next best step.

After I gave a brief explanation that a Psalm was simply Scriptural truth run through our experience we went out. I soon began to see it was a very valuable time for me and I was praying (actually, hoping and praying) that it was the same for the others. I still remember some specific lines I wrote during that hour.

When we returned, I explained I was not taking nominations for Psalm 151, nor were we judging a poetry reading, but rather inviting them to read their psalm as an expression of their praise.

By the time the second person had completed reading their psalm, we were all spontaneously prostrate on the floor in deep worship. For about 30 minutes, we all had opportunity to be more in awe of His greatness and love. No music, just deep, heart-felt, carefully crafted expressions of individual praise that we were allowed to listen in on. Even with no music involved it was a wonderful time of deep worship.

The Spirit of God loves to use the Word of God in the children of God to focus our attention on the Son of God. When this happens, real worship happens. Music can be a great enhancement, but it is not a requirement.

> ➤ **Blessed by Doing** – Ask the Lord what Scriptures and activity your prayer group could use to engage in worship without using music. Suggest that activity the next time you have opportunity.

4.3 What should be the primary focus of our prayers?

One of the most effective ways to keep our corporate prayer dynamic is to keep it focused on Jesus. Jesus and His desires is a far more long-lasting and motivating factor in our praying than us and our needs.

On several occasions Jesus let people know that He is the primary topic of Scripture. To His dissenters, Jesus said "You diligently study the Scriptures because you think that by them you possess eternal life. These are the Scriptures that testify about Me, yet you refuse to come to Me to have life" (John 5:39-40). And to His followers, Jesus, "...beginning with Moses and all the Prophets, (He) explained to them what was said in all the Scriptures concerning Himself" (Luke 24:27).

> *One of the most effective ways to keep our corporate prayer dynamic is to keep it focused on Jesus.*

Both Jesus and other biblical characters emphasize the story of the love the Father has for the Son. John the Baptist said, "The Father loves the Son and has placed everything in His hands" (John 3:35). In Ephesians 1:6 Paul adds "... which He has freely given us in the One He loves." And again in Colossians 1:13 he writes "For He has rescued us from the dominion of darkness and brought us into the kingdom of the Son He loves,..." In each of these cases, this was not the primary message, it was intentionally inserted by the author.

Jesus himself emphasized this as He taught and prayed.

- John 5:20 "For *the Father loves the Son* and shows him all he does."

- John 15:9 "As *the Father has loved me*, so have I loved you."
- John 17:24-26 "...Father, I want those you have given me to be with me where I am, and to see my glory, the glory you have given me *because you loved me* before the creation of the world. Righteous Father, though the world does not know you, I know you, and they know that you have sent me. I have made you known to them, and will continue to make you known *in order that the love you have for me* may be in them and that I myself may be in them." (Emphasis added.)

Dr. Tim Keller says, "If we ever tell a particular Bible story without putting it into the overall main Bible story (about Christ) we actually change the meaning of the particular event for us. It becomes a moralistic exhortation to 'try harder' rather than a call to live by faith in the work of Christ. There is, in the end, only two ways to read the Bible: Is it a book basically about me or basically about Jesus?"

This reflects both Spurgeon and Calvin. "From every text of Scripture there is a road to Christ. And my dear brother, your business is, when you get to the text, to say, now, what is the road to Christ? I have never found a text that did not have a road to Christ in it." (Charles Spurgeon) "We ought to read the Scriptures with the express design of finding Christ in them." (John Calvin)

Since He, and the relationship between Him and the Father, is the primary story of the Scriptures, it is also appropriate that Jesus and His kingdom be the primary object of our prayers. This is also very clear from the first three requests of the Lord's Prayer.[26]

When Jesus taught us the specific way He wanted us to pray He began with these three requests: Let Your name be holy, let Your kingdom come, and let Your will be done. It is very appropriate for us to pray about our needs. But Jesus made it very clear that before we pray about our needs, we should first consider His desires.

---

[26] See footnote 1 on page 38.

Later in the same chapter, Jesus summarizes His teaching by saying, "But seek first His kingdom and His righteousness, and all these things will be given you as well." (Matthew 6:33) It is not that we should not pray about our needs. It is that we should be aware that His kingdom has priority over our needs. If we seek Him and His righteousness, then our needs will also be met. But if all we do is seek to have our needs met in prayer, it is a real possibility that we will miss Him who is Life itself!

> *Since He, and the relationship between Him and the Father, is the primary story of the Scriptures, it is also appropriate that Jesus and His kingdom is the primary object of our prayers.*

Great saints of the past understood this. People like Count Zinzendorf, and A. B. Simpson (and many others) write that the joy of prayer is not when we seek the gifts that He can provide for us, but rather when we seek the Giver Himself.

This is what David writes about in Psalm 131:2. "But I have stilled and quieted my soul; like a weaned child with its mother, like a weaned child is my soul within me."

A weaned child is one that is no longer nursing. The reason this child is at its mother's breast is not to receive nourishment. It is not there to receive anything but the warmth of the mother's love. The picture David gives us is to help us see the absolute delight of being with Him simply to enjoy His presence. Often times we need to get to this place on purpose. We need to speak to our soul with all of its concerns and say, "Be still." We need to recalibrate at times and recognize that what looks like the most pressing need is not the most pressing need. There is a place for making requests to Him. Jesus invites us to bring Him our requests. But they are not to preempt time spent just to enjoy Him.

➤ **Blessed by Doing** – The next time you have opportunity, seek to facilitate at least half of the prayer time simply focusing on Jesus from some key Scriptures, such as Colossians 1:15-20, Philippians 2:1-11 or Revelation 4 and 5.

4.4 What keeps us from focusing on Jesus and worshiping Him in prayer?

For the typical person in the pew, prayer would probably be defined as, "Asking God for things or asking Him to do things." Too often we don't see prayer as a primary means of worship. David did. In the Psalms, much of what David wrote was an expression of praise and adoration regarding the greatness of God and His wonderful love. He sought God for who He is. But our prayers are too often about seeking God only to meet a need. How did we get here?

Unfortunately, I think people have gotten to this point because they have followed us as their spiritual leaders. In many cases, we have led them to the lowest common denominator when it comes to prayer. We have taught them that prayer is simply about asking.

Therefore, we see asking as the primary purpose of our corporate prayer. The reason people come to a time of prayer is to be prayed for or, to pray for the needs of others. This is also reflected in the primary question the prayer leader asks toward the beginning of a time of prayer. "What are your prayer requests?" It is certainly not wrong to pray for specific requests. God wants us to present our requests before Him.

But if the question, "What are your prayer requests?" is the only way we introduce our times of prayer, then those who hear it will eventually develop a faulty theology of prayer. God becomes the vending machine and our prayers become the coins. If we put the right coins in the machine, and press D-3 then we will get our answer. And if we don't get our answer we think there is something wrong with the machine.

There is so much more to prayer than this! Rather than seeing prayer as a wonderful invitation to deepen our love relationship with the God of the universe, we have come to think it is the last resort to make sure our needs are met.

But if the question, "What are your prayer requests?" is the only way we introduce our times of prayer, then those who hear it will eventually develop a faulty theology of prayer.

Continually focusing on our needs rather than on Him and His desires robs us of wonderful relationship and causes us to miss some of His best answers.

➤ **Blessed by Doing** – Intentionally don't ask for prayer requests in the next time of prayer you facilitate. Explain you are going to try an experiment. Spend time exalting Jesus then only pray about the things you sense are really on His heart.

4.5 In times of corporate prayer, how do we keep the focus on Jesus and His requests rather than on us and our requests?

As you consider how to begin a time of prayer, there are many ways to keep the focus on Jesus. One of my first memories of the first Prayer Summit I attended is of times when we began a session simply by reflecting back to Jesus some of His Scriptural names and titles. As I have facilitated times of prayer, I have often done a similar thing after singing a song about Jesus.

At a Congregational Prayer Summit in Canada we sang, "All of You is more than enough for all of me…" Coming out of that song I invited the nearly 100 people to begin sharing one by one who Jesus is to them. I encouraged them to complete the phrase, "Jesus You are my _____." People began saying, "Jesus, You are my light." "Jesus You are my rock." "Jesus, You are my conqueror."

After several minutes of this, I invited them to add to this by placing a "because" in front of the phrase and state some of the significance of the word they used to describe Jesus. So, now people were saying, "Jesus because you are my rock, I can stand on You." "Jesus, because you are my justification, I don't have to justify myself." "Jesus, because you are the way, I can walk on You knowing I will get to where I am supposed to be."

Other ways this could happen would be to invite people to complete one of the following phrases.

- Jesus, today I love You because You are _____.
- I know that You are _____.
- As my Savior You _____.
- Jesus, only You (can) _____.
- The best thing about You Jesus, is that You _____.

I want to emphasize that just because this is a simple activity, and people can enter into it rather easily, I do not see it as a trivial thing just to get people praying. In fact, I believe this could be one of the most significant means of worshiping God.

Think with me about when God first revealed Himself to Moses as, "I AM" (or "I AM WHO I AM") in Exodus 3:14. This is the name that became so sacred to the Hebrews that they did not even pronounce it. Since God revealed to Moses that His personal name is, "I AM" is there a higher response to this revelation of God than for us to stand in His presence and agree with Him? When we stand before Him and declare that "Jesus (or Father) You are _____ (insert a biblical revelation of who He is)" are we not responding to Him in a way that corresponds to that revelation? I have seen in myself and in others that this simple exercise can lead to deep times of worship.

There are many passages of Scripture that focus on Jesus. If a group is less familiar with Scripture, you may want to print out a few passages like Colossians 1:15-20, or Philippians 2:5-11, or Hebrews 1:3-4, or Revelation 1:12-16. Or if the group is more familiar with Scripture you may simply ask them to turn to a passage of Scripture or Scriptural story that describes some aspect of who Jesus is. In either case you can ask them to read the passage over a few times silently, then read it out loud to the group and pray through it, perhaps changing some of the pronouns so the passage becomes a prayer.

The first three requests of the Lord's Prayer also lend themselves to focusing on Jesus as we pray.[27] You can ask people to read over these three lines (Let Your name be holy, Let Your kingdom come, Let Your will be done) and choose one of these lines to consider for a few minutes. Then ask them to ponder the implications of this line. Point out that these are the requests that Jesus wants us to pray and encourage them to get in smaller groups, such as 3 or 4 and personalize one of these requests. So, people might pray, "Jesus, since You have stated clearly that You want Your Father's name to be holy here on earth like it is in heaven, please increase my capacity to see how His name is treated there so I can treat it like that here in my world."

I was with about eight people in a home one evening for a planning meeting. As we entered into a time in prayer I referenced the third request of the Lord's Prayer (Let Your will be done). I encouraged them to pray about any aspect of what we had been talking about but to conclude their prayer with the words, "Jesus, so that Your will will be more accomplished in our church." As we wrapped up the time of prayer, they commented that this suggestion brought a new sense of freshness and focus to the time of prayer.

These examples and suggestions may be helpful. But what helps most in seeking to keep our prayers focused on Jesus and His requests is not a specific prayer suggestion or activity. What matters most is that the facilitator continues to "fix their eyes on Jesus" during the time of prayer. If they do this and then dialogue with the Holy Spirit about how the Father wants to exalt Jesus in their midst, He will be faithful to guide them in specific ways to make this happen. Exalting Jesus is one of the favorite assignments of the Holy Spirit. So, when we ask Him how He wants to do that, He is excited to answer that prayer. And often times the answer comes in

---

[27] See footnote 1 on page 38.

a rather creative manner.

There was a time when we had completed a song about the beauty of the Lord. As we did I suggested that people tell Jesus about some aspect of His beauty they appreciate. I encouraged them to start with the words, "Jesus I see Your beauty in _____." This was a wonderful and creative time of focusing on many aspects of Jesus. Many people entered in. They prayed prayers like, "Jesus I see Your beauty in – the cross – the life of my husband – the stillness – in the morning sky – in Psalm 23 – in Your birth..."

I want to emphasize again that this did not happen because I planned in out. But rather this happened because, as I was singing about His beauty, I was also seeing with "the eyes of my heart" His beauty in different things. In my dialogue with the Holy Spirit about this, I sensed His direction to invite the other people into what I was already doing. It was His creative suggestion at just the right moment that allowed people to flow into this time of worship.

As you facilitate times of corporate prayer, listen to what is being sung, read, or prayed. Interact with the Holy Spirit about it. Ask Him how these truths could be prayed. Then don't be afraid of His creativity. Be willing to try a new approach.

> **Blessed by Doing** – Be willing to try a new approach during your next time of prayer. Look over the answer above and either suggest something I have written here, or (better yet) ask the Lord for a fresh way to focus on Jesus and His requests.

United and Ignited

5. Scripture – What is the role of Scripture in facilitating dynamic corporate prayer?

One of the reasons corporate prayer is dynamic is because it flows from Scripture which is described in Hebrews 4:12 as being "... alive and powerful." It is His Word that is, "... inspired by God and profitable..." (2 Timothy 3:16). His Word gives life and light and creative power. Our temporal words are significant only as they are in agreement with His eternal Word. So, as we pray, to the degree we rely upon and pray back to Him His words, to that same degree we can pray with confidence and clarity. The use of Scripture as we pray will change our praying. Instead of praying from human knowledge, we will be praying with divine wisdom.

In fact the more I pray, the more I feel the need to have my prayers based upon and reflect Scripture. My default setting is still very self-centered prayers. I need His Word and His perspective to keep me away from coming to prayer with the thought that it is all about me. And I have yet to find a need that could not be addressed in prayer from Scripture.

So, as you facilitate corporate prayer, encourage the pray-ers to always bring their Bibles with them. You may want to make sure that there are some extra Bibles available. I have often quipped, "If I see that you don't have your Bible with you, I will assume you have it memorized. Then I will ask you to stand and quote the book of Obadiah."

Because the best prayer is based upon Scripture, your commitment to spend regular time hearing, reading, studying, memorizing, and meditating upon it will be one of the best ways you can improve your ability to facilitate dynamic corporate prayer. This is not a short-term process. It is a life-long journey. Don't be satisfied with your present level of Scriptural intake. Press on. Make use of every opportunity to know His Word better. It will pay great dividends not only as you facilitate prayer but in all the other areas of your life as well.

> *Your commitment to spend regular time hearing, reading, studying, memorizing, and meditating upon it will be one of the best ways you can improve your ability to facilitate dynamic corporate prayer.*

➢ **Blessed by Doing** – Encourage people in your prayer group to make it a habit to bring their Bibles to the time of prayer. Also, if possible, have some extra copies available.

➢ **Blessed by Doing** – Refresh your own commitment to get as much of His Word into your mind and heart as possible.

5.1 Can we pray from just one verse?

There are times when the Lord may direct you to have an entire session of prayer around just one verse, or a couple verses. There are a variety of ways this could happen, so the examples I will give you are just that, examples. Please be sensitive to the Holy Spirit in your setting so you have a confidence you are following His leadership.

We often hear people pray the phrase from the Lord's Prayer, "Lord, let Your kingdom come." This is a great line and a great prayer. But what if we took the time to explore and expand the idea of His Kingdom? What does it look like? Can we pray more specifically than just, "Let Your kingdom come?"

I have facilitated sessions of prayer around just one verse that helps us answer some of these questions. In Romans 14:17 the Holy Spirit through Paul says, "The kingdom of God is not eating or drinking, but righteousness, peace, and joy in the Holy Spirit." Here is a specific, Biblical definition of the Kingdom of God. It consists

Scripture

of righteousness, peace, and joy. Each of these three qualities comes from the Holy Spirit.

So, in praying for His kingdom to come, we could pray for each of these traits in particular. A question I have asked a group of pray-ers is "Who or what in your neighborhood (or city, or school, or workplace, or family) needs more of God's righteousness?" After I get some responses – and perhaps write them on a white board – I have invited them to get in smaller groups of 3 or 4 and pray that the Kingdom of God (specifically His righteousness) would come to these people or places. I have found that when they are able to pray with a reminder of what the kingdom looks like and how it could come to a person or a group of people, a fresh energy of prayer is released. This same pattern could be done with peace and joy. If we took a few minutes to consider each of these kingdom traits – then a few minutes to pray from each one of them – that could make a very powerful time of corporate prayer.

There are many other individual verses (or a set of verses) that lend themselves to a time of corporate prayer. 2 Chronicles 7:14, Romans 12:1-2, Romans 15:13, Galatians 5:22-23, 1 Thessalonians 5:16-18, 2 Thessalonians 3:1-2, Revelation 5:12 or 13 are just a few of the verses that could be the focus of a time of corporate prayer.

> **Blessed by Doing** – Facilitate a time of prayer based upon one of the verses above or another verse you sense the Holy Spirit has directed you to.

5.2 How can we pray through a large section of Scripture?

Another way we can use Scripture is to pray through a chapter or even an entire book. Obviously, this will take more time than praying through a small portion, but there can be great impact from it. This could be done in a multi-day prayer setting, or weekly time of prayer.

While leading a time of prayer on the Hood Canal in Washington State, I sensed we were to pray from Isaiah 40. I was familiar with this wonderful chapter and how it contains many aspects of God's character and heart. As I was considering how we might be able to cover the entire chapter, I saw the connection between the 31 verses in the chapter and that each person in the room had a birth date that was between the number 1 and 31. So, I asked people to go to the verse in the chapter that matched the day of their birth. Then I invited them to start with that verse and read, "till you find a truth about God worth reflecting upon. Ponder that truth and spend time in prayer around that truth." I gave them a few minutes to read and pray in silence then asked them to, "do together, out loud, what we were doing individually in silence." God met us in a very meaningful way.

For example, one person prayed from verse one. [Comfort, comfort my people, says your God.] "Thank You that You are a God who brings comfort to Your people! I remember how You have brought me comfort in my time of need." From verse 5 [And the glory of the Lord will be revealed, and all mankind together will see it. For the mouth of the LORD has spoken.] someone prayed, "Father, let me see the glory You have revealed around me. Let me and all mankind see it and worship You. And thank You that when You speak, it will happen. Thank You that Your Word will be accomplished." Jesus received much praise and adoration during that time. And from these verses, many confident prayers of petition and intercession took place.

The second night of a Prayer Summit in Tucson, AZ. I invited three pastors to read through 1 Thessalonians 2:1-13 out loud from three different versions. After the first reading I mentioned that this passage of Scripture contained many key ministry principles from Paul's life. I then invited the men to listen for these principles and after the last reading to begin praying these principles into one another's lives. When the third reading was complete, one man got up, knelt down in front of another man and began to pray his heart out for this dear brother. Soon others joined him. The end result was over two hours of uninterrupted prayer that was based upon Scripture and coming from deep within the hearts of the pray-ers.

Everyone left that time of prayer knowing the power of the Scriptures in a fresh way.

I have been in prayer times when we have prayed through a chapter, a few chapters (such as Matthew 5-7 or John 14-16) as well as entire books (like Philippians, or Colossians) and each time God's Word has been shown to be both, "alive and powerful."

Reading larger portions of Scripture out loud can also be very edifying. On several occasions I have been with a group that has read the entire book of Revelation in one sitting. The instructions were simple. This book promises a blessing to those who read and to those who hear. The name of this book is "The Revelation of Jesus Christ." I have asked people to notice the big themes of the book as each person read one chapter out loud in a manner that reflects what is happening in the text. At times we have prayed a brief prayer at the end of each chapter. By the time we are at the end, there is a clear sense of the Greatness of Jesus, the horror of sin, and the assurance of promised victory!

At other times I have encouraged people to read without comment or prayer, Scriptures on a specific theme that became evident as we prayed, such as grace, humility, His promises, His greatness, or His faithfulness. As we hear verse after verse read out loud, it does what Paul describes in Ephesians 5:26. It "Cleanses (us) by the washing of the water through the word…"

> *On several occasions I have been with a group that has read the entire book of Revelation in one sitting.*

- ➢ **Blessed by Doing** – Select a chapter or two from Scripture and encourage your prayer group to pray from it. Have the group read it through a couple times noticing truths they could pray from. Then ask them to pray those truths.

5.3 How can we pray through certain topics of Scripture?

There were about 25 pastors gathered in a simple chapel at Warm Beach Camp in Washington State. The West side of the chapel was all glass. It overlooked the Puget Sound and the Olympic mountains. It was 7:00am. This was a bonus session on the last day of a three day Prayer Summit.

Over the years I have gathered verses on the topic of what God has for us or wants from us in, the *morning*. There was no place to write out these references in the chapel, so as they entered, I just assigned each pastor a verse. I asked them to read over the verse a few times, consider what it says about the morning and then to form a prayer about what it says. After a few minutes, I encouraged them to begin praying out loud. What a refreshing time of meeting with the Lord and these brothers!

I have come to call this, *concordance praying* because it is very easy to develop a list of references on a topic from a concordance. Prayers about grace, the kingdom of God, Scripture, His love, are just a few of the topics that can be prayed through in this manner. In preparation for sharing in the Lord's Supper, a very meaningful way to pray is to pray Scriptures specifically about the cross.

There are times when I have written references on a white board, distributed them on a piece of paper, assigned each person a verse or just asked people to use their memories to develop a list as we are praying. In each case the simple instruction is to read the verse over a few times, note what the verse says about the specific topic, then turn it into a prayer. There have been times when I have encouraged one person to pray from their verse and then have two or three others to add their prayers from the same verse.

The point is not in the specific directives but rather in being sensitive to the Lord so He can be the real facilitator of the time of prayer.

➤ **Blessed by Doing** – Develop a list of verses from a specific Scriptural topic, such as His grace, mercy, love, greatness, or holiness. Facilitate a time of prayer based upon these verses. For more examples of this, go to the resources page at

www.uandibook.net.

5.4 How can we pray from specific Scriptural prayers?

Perhaps one of the most obvious ways that we can pray from Scripture is by praying through specific prayers that are already there. Much of the book of Psalms is already in the form of a prayer. So, just reading through them carefully and prayerfully can be a very meaningful time of corporate prayer.

I have had the opportunity to be in Israel on a few occasions. One of my best memories is standing at Qumran in view of cave number 4 where many of the Dead Sea Scrolls were found and reading through Psalm 119 as a prayer. It is not only the longest chapter in the Bible, it is the longest prayer in the Bible. It becomes a prayer in verse 4. And the topic of the entire Psalm is David's radical love for God's law. So, under some make shift shade guarding us from the scorching sun, we read the entire Psalm verse by verse and prayed each word we said. There is no place on earth that better demonstrates God's commitment to preserve His Word than that cave. So, as a group of us stood in the hot Qumran sun reading and praying through Psalm 119 we not only had a clearer sense of what David was writing about, we also had a wonderful time of Scripture-based prayer.

Other Old Testament prayers that can provide an outline for a time of dynamic corporate prayer are Moses' conversation with the Lord (Exodus 33:12-23), David's prayers of thanks (1 Chronicles 16 and 17), Elijah's prayer on Mt. Carmel (1 Kings 18:36-37), and the prayers of Ezra, Nehemiah, and Daniel (see chapter 9 of their books).

Paul's prayers for the churches he loved are also great patterns for our prayers. His six primary prayers for churches (Ephesians 1:15-23, 3:14-21, Philippians 1:9-11, Colossians 1:9-14, 1 Thessalonians 3:11-13, and 2 Thessalonians 1:11-12) can each be used individually as great models for a time of prayer. But it is also a very powerful time to look at all six of these prayers.

Prior to a Prayer Summit, I had noticed both the topics and themes of these six prayers. I found 5 major themes of these prayers. I also found fresh faith as I prayed through them. So, at one point in the summit, I gave the pastors a page containing these six prayers in columns on a single page and asked them to get alone and notice the topics and the themes of these prayers. When we returned about a half hour later, I invited the pastors to pray, "like Paul prayed" for the Church of their city. Later I asked them to pray in a similar manner for one another. This provided these men a great opportunity to express their heart for their city through prayer and to pray with a high level of confidence that they were praying the way God wanted them to pray.

> *I gave the pastors a page containing these six prayers in columns on a single page and asked them to get alone and notice the topics and the themes of these prayers.*

Of course, Jesus' prayers provide the best model for our prayers. We so often slide right over the top of the Lord's Prayer because it is so familiar to us. It has lost nearly all of its impact because we have not taken it as seriously as Jesus meant for us to take it.

Let me point out two things about the value of this prayer. First of all, these are not haphazard words patched together at the last minute because Jesus was caught off guard when He was asked to teach His disciples to pray. Indeed, they are the very thought-through words of the infinite God, in human flesh, on this essential topic of prayer. This is God's best instruction to those of us who want to learn to pray more and more effectively. Second, this is spoken by Jesus in the plural. He did not teach us to pray to "my" Father but to "our" Father. He instructed us to pray for "our" needs, "our" forgiveness, "our" guidance, and "our" deliverance. When it comes to corporate prayer, I am convinced that Jesus had much more in mind than us simply reciting this prayer in unison.

After giving a little instruction on the way this prayer could be used in corporate prayer at a three-day Congregational Prayer Summit, the prayer pastor of the church led us in a wonderful season of prayer. It is worth describing in more detail.

I shared briefly that I love to pray from the two halves of the Lord's Prayer. There is the "Your" half – "may Your name be holy, may Your kingdom come, and may Your will be done." Then there is the "us" half – "give us, forgive us, lead us and deliver us." These two halves can be prayed through separately. But I believe there is a clear connection between the two. The first half contains Jesus' three primary requests. The second half reflects all of man's needs.

I went on to explain that once when I was praying through these seven requests, I found myself praying through each request of the first half, then when I came to the fourth request, something happened that significantly changed the way I pray. I prayed like this. "Father, now please give me what I need today (my daily bread) so that Your name will be more holy on earth like it is in heaven. And give me what I need so that Your kingdom will be advanced through my life today. And please give me the things I need to both know and accomplish Your will." I went on to pray in a similar manner through each of the four requests of the second half of the prayer. Adding the *so that* and pointing the request back to His name, His kingdom, and His will elevated the significance of my prayers.

After this instruction my friend Ezra, the prayer pastor, led the group in a season of prayer where we prayed through the four requests of the second half, but always added a *so that* and finished our prayers with one of the three requests of the first half. I left this time of prayer feeling like I had never prayed more effectively for a congregation.

Praying around Jesus' prayer recorded in John 17 has also sharpened times of group pray. His four requests – Father, glorify Your Son (v. 1&5), protect them (v. 11&15), sanctify them (v. 17) and unite them (v. 11, 21&23) provide a wonderful and divine pattern for us to pray for the people we care about. Leaders can easily, and should, follow this pattern as they pray for the people under their care.

➢ **Blessed by Doing** – Select a Scriptural prayer (whether men-tioned above or not) and facilitate a time of prayer around it. Ask the Holy Spirit for guidance and also *test drive* the prayer in your own personal time of prayer. For other helpful resources, go to www.uandibook.net.

> *I left this time of prayer feeling like I had never prayed more effectively for a congregation.*

5.5 How can meditation enhance times of corporate pray-er?

Of all the ways we can interact with Scripture, meditation is by far the most valuable. A simple study of the word *meditation* in Scripture can give you a good understanding of both its value and how to engage in Biblical meditation. Chapter 2 of *Living Prayer: The Lord's Prayer Alive in You* addresses this most helpful process.

Let me list three quick points here.

Meditation cannot be done quickly. The nature of the process requires that we slow down and ponder the words before us.

Meditation engages both the mind and the heart. It is not only thinking slowly through a text, it is also setting your heart on receiving the nourishment and health inherently contained in the text.

Finally, to fully receive the benefit of meditation it must include heart to Heart dialogue with the Author. Meditation must lead us to prayer.

With this in mind, a way to glean the truths from Scripture and to help us pray through Scripture most effectively in a group setting is to give people a little direction and time so they can meditate on it personally first.

I remember a time when we divided the people into four groups. Each group selected a chapter of Colossians from which to meditate for a period of time. The goal was not to simply read through the chapter, but to meditate on a few verses from the chapter with the anticipation that when we returned together we would use that as the basis of our time of corporate prayer.

When we returned in about an hour, it was a very rich time of worship and prayer as people prayed back to God deep insights He had opened up to them. We were not in a hurry and we were not trying to impress each other with our knowledge. We were taking time to interact with our Lord around His Word. As we did, it was evident that we had encountered God personally and now that encounter was expanding to include all the others in the room.

Meditation can also take place together. Many times in a corporate setting, we have looked at a passage of Scripture and used it as the basis of our times of prayer. There is a perking of life that takes place as the children of God allow the Spirit of God to use the Word of God to shape their prayers.

I remember the depth and the heart-felt repentance of pastors as we meditated and prayed through the story of Mary and Martha in Luke 10:38-42. People prayed about the distractions of ministry, of life, of poor relationships, and worries. They identified with Martha's desire to be a good hostess that turned into self-pity and even giving Jesus a command to have Mary come help her. We recognized the value of the simple thing of sitting at Jesus' feet, listening, and hanging on every word He said. After we began with this passage we prayed from other, related passages. This passage allowed us to touch God and Him to touch us as we took time to think slowly through this passage together.

As we did, it was evident that we had encountered God personally and now that encounter was expanding to include all the others in the room.

Because we were doing this together, the end result was much more than any one of us could have gleaned individually.

➢ **Blessed by Doing** – Develop the habit of meditating on Scripture as you pray. As you facilitate a time of prayer, encourage the pray-ers to take personal time to meditate on a certain passage of Scripture. When the group is familiar with meditation, you may want to do this as a group.

6. Preparation – What is the role of the facilitator before a session of prayer?

What the facilitator does before facilitating a time of prayer will greatly determine the level of prayer during that session. It will determine how deeply people connect with God. It will determine how people think and talk about that time of prayer after the session is over. Just as an airline pilot would never consider just waking up, getting dressed, slipping into the cockpit, and starting down the runway, so also a skilled prayer facilitator will give attention to several aspects of the time of prayer before it is time to start the session.

6.1 How can I prepare a room for dynamic corporate prayer?

The way a room is set up can have a great bearing on the depth of the prayer that happens there. This is not the most important factor, but it is a factor. You want to remove as many distractions as possible. Generally speaking, try to find a room that is the right size for your group. Also, because hearing one another is important, the best arrangement in most cases would be to form the chairs in a circle or concentric circles.

If it is a larger group, it works well to have the inner circle have about 20- 30 chairs. There does not need to be a "front" with a podium, etc. because the facilitator(s) should sit with the others. In fact, there is value in the facilitator moving from place to place for different sessions so no "front" develops. The chairs should have a little space between them and there should be a few aisles so people can get to each chair fairly easily.

If there is a reason to set the room up differently then don't be bound by this. Your time of prayer may lend itself to having no chairs for a session, or chairs set in a certain location to depict (for example) the tabernacle, or set around tables, or in a retreat setting around a fireplace, etc. You may want to start a session with people in small groups, so setting the chairs in that manner will make that happen smoothly.

You will also want to think through the noise factor and the heat factor. Will the furnace or air conditioner or some other machine (like a lawn mower) be a distraction? A room that is too warm will cause people to drift off. A room that is too cold will cause people to only be thinking about how they can warm up. The key is to think this through and have a reason for how you set up the room. As much as possible let the room arrangement be your servant. Let it serve your (and the Lord's) purposes.

➤ **Blessed by Doing** – consider the physical arrangement of the room where your group prays. Should you make any adjustment to make it more conducive to prayer?

6.2 How can I prepare my heart before I facilitate a time of dynamic corporate prayer?

As I have opportunity to facilitate a time of corporate prayer, I am never very far from thinking about that time of prayer and what the Lord might want to do during it. If, in fact, that time of prayer has the possibility to help those in the group connect with and encounter God in a more meaningful way, if this is an opportunity to see more of heaven affect earth, then I have a huge responsibility and opportunity before me. I always take it as seriously, as seriously as if I were to preach or teach.

In addition to the things I do just prior to the time of prayer, here are some things I do even when the time of prayer is days or weeks away. (For what I do just prior to the time of prayer see Question 6.3) I try to live a surrendered life all the time. But as I consider facilitating a time of prayer, I specifically surrender my heart, mind, desires, thoughts, and motives to Him so He is able to use me any way He might choose. I spend time praying for the people who will be coming. I pray that God's desired outcomes would take place as a result of this time of prayer.

I also take time to pray and specifically ask the Lord for His direction for the time. I always ask Him to lead the time through me or through someone else. The interesting thing about this prayer is that He rarely answers it when I pray it or how I anticipate He will answer it. It is not like a conversation with another human. In that setting the communication flows. I speak, they listen. They speak, I listen. Their words relate to my words.

But I have found it is not like that with God. I speak, He listens... but often doesn't say anything right then. Later, when I am not thinking about it at all, and often not expecting it, He speaks. The key thing at that point is for me to listen, and make a note of it.

For example, after I have prayed about my role in a time of prayer I may be driving, or engaged in a conversation with a friend, or watching TV, or reading, or studying another topic. Then, there is a clear thought about (for example) some aspect of God's wonderful grace. And I sense there is a connection between that thought and the time of prayer I am scheduled to facilitate.

> *The interesting thing about this prayer is that He rarely answers it when I pray it or how I anticipate He will answer it.*

Or, I may sense Him say, "When you are with _____ (a certain group) I want you to start the time of prayer by focusing on My grace." Most often, I am not thinking about that specific time of prayer, but the Lord nudges me to use that thought with that group.

I always ask for sensitivity to the Holy Spirit, that I might see and fan what He is doing. Since the Holy Spirit is the best facilitator of prayer – according to Romans 8:26 He helps us to pray – it is essential to seek to be sensitive to His leading as we lead. He is that "still, small voice." Scripture says He comes in the form of a dove. When doves land, they land in places without a lot of com-

① The Holy Spirit 89 himself intercedes for us...that words cannot express

motion. The same is true with the Holy Spirit. He comes to the person whose spirit is calm enough for Him to find a place to land. So, I seek to quiet my heart before Him. As we seek Him and trust Him, He will be very faithful to lead us.

In addition to specific surrender and specific prayer, there is one other thing I do on a regular basis. When I read, hear, or study Scripture, I am most always asking the question, "How could this truth be prayed?" In the same way many preachers or teachers are always asking the question of Scripture, "How could this text preach?" I am asking, "How could this text pray?" It is important to note that my question is not simply about how I might lead others in prayer from this verse, but rather how can I pray from it. Sometimes as I prepare to facilitate, the Lord may remind me of a way I have prayed from Scripture and I sense I am to invite others into it, but that is not the primary reason I do this. I do it because I want to use every opportunity to pray and press into the Lord.

While writing this section, I randomly opened my Bible to illustrate how this might work. I opened to the Triumphal Entry passage in John 12: 12-15. As I asked the question, "How could this passage pray?" a thought that came to me from v. 13. It says, "Blessed is He who comes in the name of the Lord." In addition to Him coming in the name of the Lord, Jesus also does other things. So, a way I could pray from this verse is, "Blessed are You who saves me, in the name of the Lord." Or, "Blessed are You who has created all I see and all there is, in the name of the Lord." Or, "Blessed are You who will keep me from the evil one, in the name of the Lord."

> *In the same way many preachers or teachers are always asking the question of Scripture, "How could this text preach?" I am asking, "How could this text pray?"*

Because I have made a habit of doing this when I am not thinking or preparing for a specific time of prayer, I have found it comes very naturally to me when I am considering or even facilitating a time of prayer.

> **Blessed by Doing** – Begin to practice what I wrote above about asking how a truth from a song or from the Scriptures can be prayed. Do this often, until it becomes second nature to you.
> **Blessed by Doing** – Also be intentional about preparing your heart before the Lord before you facilitate your next time of prayer.

6.3 How can I prepare to start a specific time of dynamic corporate prayer?

This is what I normally do before I begin a time of prayer. The Lord may lead you in an entirely different manner. I would not say there is a universal, *best* way to prepare. I would say, however, that it is vitally important that you take time to go through a process so that you are confident both your heart and your mind are prepared.

Before each session of prayer I always try to get by myself or with another leader or facilitator for about 15 or more minutes. If I am by myself, I first take time just to enjoy God for Who He is. As the song says, I take time to, "tune my heart to sing Thy praise." Often I will read, meditate, and pray through some Scriptures, sing songs which allow me to see His greatness and glory. During this time, I am not necessarily considering how the time of prayer should develop. I am just enjoying Him. Sometimes I pray for individuals I know who will be in the prayer group, that they would be impacted in a special way.

If, prior to this time, I have a sense of how we are to begin, I present that idea before the Lord for confirmation. If I do not have a specific sense as to how we should begin, and if this is a group that meets on an ongoing basis, I reflect on how we were praying the last time we were together. Sometimes the Lord will remind me of something that may have been unfinished and it is right for us to return to that topic. At other times I just dialogue with the Lord about what we could do. I consider passages of Scripture that have been *life* to me recently. Sometimes that is where we go.

If I am with another person who has leadership responsibilities in this group, we often have a time of prayer asking for God's clear direction. We will then share with each other if or what direction we may want to consider. We may talk about some specific passages of Scripture and consider if they may be helpful. And we also express to God and each other our dependence upon Him for this time as well as our willingness to go where He may lead us.

As I consider the different thoughts, some weigh more (or fit better) than others. Sometimes there is only one really clear thought. That makes it easier. Sometimes I (or we) have to decide what we think the Lord wants us to do. I try to think through the starting point and see how well I could follow the suggestions I am considering giving to others. If they don't work well for me, chances are good we don't want to go there. And there is a point at which it is very appropriate to do that which seems obvious or best.

Sometimes all I know is that we are to start with a specific song, or Scripture passage. Sometimes it is just a word like, "forgive," or "exalt." I have facilitated sessions of prayer that were entirely tethered to just one idea. We began and together we caught the flow of what God wanted to accomplish. Other times I have sensed I am to set the scene by sharing some very brief thoughts from a passage of Scripture and a suggested starting point.

Once, after I had been impressed with some of the "one things" of Scripture (see for example Ps. 27:4, Luke 10: 42, and Phil, 3:13), I shared a few minutes introducing this thought to a group of pastors and encouraged them to get together in groups of 5 or 6 and each one pray from one or more of these passages. With less 5 minutes worth of instruction, some of these groups took up to two hours in prayer. And, in this setting, the groups that prayed the longest enjoyed it the most.

Other times the starting time approaches and I do not have a clear direction. When this happens, it gives me an opportunity to walk in faith. It is always rather uncomfortable to seemingly be completely unprepared, but some of the best times of prayer have come when I had no idea how we were to proceed.

We should never use the following comments as a cop-out for lack of preparation, but perhaps one of the best ways to begin a time of prayer is to simply say something like the following. "Let's just take some time to turn our hearts toward the Lord as we begin and see how He would lead us. So, let's take some time in silence before Him. Consider Him. Then, if there is a passage of Scripture or a song on your heart, I invite you lead out with that. Let's each of us be sensitive to how the Lord wants to lead us in this time of prayer with the confidence that He has wonderful things He wants to do in our midst. So, open your hearts, open your spirits, and open your Bibles and let's see what the Lord has for us."

I have found it is always important for me to take time beforehand to interact with the Lord. Many times He makes a starting point clear. Many times He doesn't. But as we submit our minds, hearts, and spirits to Him, He proves over and over that He really is the best prayer facilitator. It is wonderful that He lets us come along with Him.

➢ **Blessed by Doing** – Develop the habit of regularly setting aside time just prior to facilitating a time of corporate prayer. Spend time enjoying Jesus and listening to the Holy Spirit for any specific direction He may want to give.

6.4 What perspectives should I have in order to facilitate dynamic corporate prayer?

If we are going to be most effective in facilitating times of corporate prayer, there are four personal perspectives we need to embrace.

6.4.1 Is it about more than prayer?

First, we need to understand that more prayer or even better prayer is not the primary goal. It is instead, the vehicle toward the goal of greater relationship with Jesus and His Body. If we seek to motivate and facilitate prayer from the perspective that more or better prayer, in and of itself, is the desired goal, we may find some, but limited success. But if we see that a deeper relationship with Jesus, a deeper awareness of all that He is, is the driving force behind more and better prayer, we will not only be able to get there ourselves, but we will also be able to help many other people reach that goal as well.

One of the most famous prayer meetings in church history is the prayer meeting that lasted more than one hundred years and was responsible for the modern missionary movement. Count Ludwig Von Zinzendorf was the founder of the Moravian movement from which the one hundred year prayer meeting took place. He was not caught up simply with the process of prayer. He was caught up with Jesus! His deep passion was to know and proclaim the value of the wounds and the blood of the wonderful Son of God. His life, travels, preaching, and praying all flowed out of that primary passion.

If we seek to motivate and facilitate prayer from the perspective that more or better prayer, in and of itself is the desired goal, we may find some, but limited success.

The same could be said of Jonathan Edwards, who was the man most responsible for the first Great Awakening in America. His passion was to see Jesus exalted in every possible way. Prayer was (and is) a key practice to accomplish that.

I have had the privilege of being around some very seasoned saints. Some who had walked with Jesus for as much as 75 years. These dear, godly people were committed to regular times of deep and meaningful prayer. But my observation is that their times in prayer were not only about the act of praying. That seemed to be the vehicle they used to get them to where they really longed to be; closer to the Savior. It was their love for the Savior that led them to a deep commitment to prayer.

The prospect of providing this rebellious human race with a deep relationship with the Father is what motivated Jesus to go to the cross. The reason Jesus left heaven, endured the rejection of His creatures, and suffered unimaginable agony on the cross was not simply so we would have our sins forgiven and could go to Heaven instead of Hell. Nor was it so He could have more people to accomplish His mission on earth. The reason why He did these things was so we could have a relationship with the Father. The forgiveness of our sins and the change of our destiny is a wonderful part of the package, and joining Him in His mission brings fulfillment in our lives, but according to John 17:3 the primary description of eternal life is a relationship with the Father and the Son.

I have been able to watch a shift take place in pastors' lives as I have facilitated Prayer Summits. Often times when pastors hear about attending a 3 or 4 day Prayer Summit, one of their first questions is "How in the world will we do nothing but pray for 3 or 4 days?" Many times I have heard pastors pray a prayer of deep repentance as they enter into the Spirit-directed flow of corporate worship and prayer. A typical prayer would be something like, "Father, please forgive me for having my priorities out of place. You first called me to Yourself, then you called me to ministry. Father, in the pressure of ministry, I have acted as though I was called to preaching (or praying or counseling) more than to You. I ask you to forgive me and I ask you to help me live as though my first priority is to live in healthy relationship with You."

This is consistent with the Apostle Paul's perspective. He prayed, "… so that you may know Him better…" (Ephesians 1:17) and, "…so that Christ may dwell in your hearts through faith…" (Ephesians 3:17) and, "…so that the name of our Lord Jesus Christ may be glorified in you…" (2 Thessalonians 1:12). His passion is summed up when he said, "…I want to know Christ" (Philippians 3:10).

To the degree that we understand and direct our prayers after the primary purpose of a deeper relationship with the Father and the

Son, to that same degree we will enhance both our times of prayer and the times of those we influence.

What about the requests and needs? I have observed that if we focus on the relational aspect of prayer, then He is able to bring up the specific requests and needs that are on His heart. Then, when we pray according to His heart, we can pray with greater confidence and see greater results. In fact, this is what Jesus taught in Matthew 6:33. If we seek His kingdom and His righteousness, then all "these things" (the real concerns of this world from verses 19-32) will be taken care of as well.

➢ **Blessed by Doing** – If you facilitate a time of prayer, begin to help those who attend develop the perspective described in the answer above. Few things will refresh your time of prayer more than this.

6.4.2 Do you, personally, embrace the value of corporate prayer?

We give ourselves to things we see as valuable. If we are going to be used by God in meaningful corporate prayer, the second perspective we must embrace is the value of the corporate prayer experience. The level of our capacity to facilitate corporate prayer well is directly tied to how much we *value* it. If we value it highly, we will take and make opportunities to engage in it and help others to engage in it.

> *The level of our capacity to facilitate corporate prayer well is directly tied to how much we value it.*

Oftentimes, our experience, and the experience of others, has not convinced us that corporate prayer has value. If we are not convinced, it will be hard to convince others. If we see the value of praying with others, they will sense this and want to join in. But once someone experiences *dynamic* corporate prayer, and sees the difference it has and can make in people's lives, they will then have the possibility of helping others find the same experience.

> **Blessed by Doing** – Consider again the corporate prayer examples from Scripture in Question 1.9. No matter what your present commitment to the value of corporate prayer, ask the Lord to strengthen and increase it.

6.4.3 Do you embrace the importance of the facilitation process?

When we have a clear perspective that the primary goal of prayer is to know God better and we also embrace the value of praying together, the next needed personal perspective is to embrace the importance of the facilitating process and the role of the facilitator.

The most important human ingredient in a meaningful time of corporate prayer is the facilitator.   Obviously, the divine factor overrides all the other ingredients. But just as the most important human ingredient in preaching is the preacher and the most important human ingredient in a worship service is the worship leader, so it is with the one leading prayer. And just like the preacher and the worship leader give themselves to prayerful and diligent preparation for their parts, so also the one who facilitates prayer not only plays the key role in the time of prayer but must also give him/herself to the same kind of diligent and prayerful preparation. If we see this as a key part of the discipleship process, we will take it seriously. We will ponder it, pray about it, practice it, and process how to do it best. See Questions 6.2 and 6.3 for more on how a facilitator can be prepared.

...the next needed personal perspective is to embrace the importance of the facilitating process and the role of the facilitator.

In preaching, the phrase "A mist in

the pulpit is a fog in the pew" emphasizes the need for clear thinking as a result of clear preparation as one preaches. And if there is a "fog in the pew" it is because the preacher has not done his job to think through each point clearly. In a similar manner, if the pray-er in the pew does not have a clear sense of how they can and should enter into the time of prayer, that is not the fault of the pray-er as much as it is the fault of the one facilitating that time of prayer.

> **Blessed by Doing** – Tell the Lord you want to see the responsibility of facilitating corporate prayer as seriously as He does. Ask the Lord to help you ponder, pray about, practice, and process how to do it in the best possible manner.

6.4.4 Are you entering the time of prayer with a desire to deepen your own relationship with Jesus?

Finally, we must approach the time with a desire to deepen our own relationship with Jesus. We must have a personal desire to exalt Him in worship. This can't simply be about helping others. If we do not see our own personal need to press into the Lord and grow in our own personal relationship with the Savior, it will be easy for us to think we are facilitating prayer simply as an exercise to benefit others. But if we have a true, heart-felt desire to come before His throne with others, so that we personally can be more conformed to His image and give Him more of the worship He deserves, we will be more qualified to help others get there too. As with many other things we do, it can't be only pointing the way, it must be leading the way. See also Questions 4.4, 4.5 and 6.4.1 above.

> **Blessed by Doing** – Ask the Lord to always help you have a hungry heart for more of Him! Then, as you facilitate corporate prayer, that will be obvious.

6.5 What are some essential traits a facilitator should possess?

On various occasions I have asked those who facilitate dynamic corporate prayer what traits are necessary to be a good facilitator. The following are some of their answers. They deserve our careful consideration.

- Be a person of prayer;
- Be a worshipper;
- Be spiritually mature and healthy
- Be a partaker of God's presence without losing perspective of the role of the facilitator;
- Have a heart in tune with God's heart;
- Walk in humility before the Lord and others;
- Understand the dynamics of various sized groups;
- Have and exercise discernment;
- Be a good listener to the Lord and those around him;
- Be able to follow the flow yet remain focused;
- Be able to remain alert;
- Be willing to risk
- Be teachable;
- Deal with criticism in a healthy manner;
- Constantly be aware of the atmosphere: the spiritual climate or environment;
- Be able to differentiate between God's work in an individual and God's movement in the group;
- Be a team player.

➢ **Blessed by Doing** – As you look over the traits above, mark three that are well established in your life and three that you would like to see more established. Ask God to strengthen you in the last three you mentioned.

6.6 How can we prepare a group as we begin a time of prayer?

It is not only the facilitators who need to be prepared for a time of meaningful prayer, it is also the group itself. Most of the time I do not know all of the participants when I lead a time of prayer. And often they don't know everyone else in the room. Therefore, a time of introduction can be helpful. I see this as part of the prayer time (not just a functional thing) so I seek the Lord on how this should happen as well.

I will often use the introduction time to help us find out some information we otherwise would not know. For example, "Please tell us where you lived when you were 10 years old and how long you have lived in your present house." The purpose of this is to help them get more at ease as well as it helps me to get to know them a bit more.

There are times when I have tied Scripture or a song to this introduction process. You may want to ask them to share a key verse of Scripture or song that has been very meaningful to them as well. In Question 6.7 below there is an example of how this can be tied into a time of prayer.

There are also three key prayers that, when prayed, have saved us many hours of unproductive prayer. They can be prayed by several people, just one person, or in some other manner.

- We pray for God's *protection* – over the time of prayer, over our loved ones so we are not distracted in any way, and over our own hearts that we would be responsive to God.
- We pray for *direction* – that we would all sense the direction He wants us to go and that we would follow Him well.
- We pray for a clear sense of His *manifest presence* – more than anything else, this is what we need and ultimately, this is what we want.

Depending on the setting, it is also good to share some "ground rules" so everyone is on the same page. This includes the value of listening (from Question 7.2 below) as well as a desire to honor one another as we pray. Sharing about the value of equal participation is also very helpful. (See Question 6.7 below.) Our desire is that all would feel comfortable to lead out in prayer and none would dominate.

Finally, I also request that name tags are used (with just their first names written in large letters) if I don't know the people in the group, so I can address each person by their name. See also 1.8 above.

➤ **Blessed by Doing** – Whether you pray with the same group regularly or with a brand new group, pray and consider what can happen prior to the prayer meeting that will enhance the time of prayer.

6.7 How can we encourage *equal participation* in prayer? That is, how can we encourage those who normally do not pray out loud to do so and how can we encourage those who normally do pray out loud to do so less?

Equal participation in prayer is a very worthy goal. This is the key truth Jesus quotes from Isaiah when He says, "My house shall be called a house of prayer *for all nations*" (Mark 11:17 and Isaiah 56:7 – emphasis added). The context of Isaiah 56 makes it clear that this is not referring to a place where all the nations are prayed for. It is referring to a place where all the nations (ethnic groups) have equal access to God in prayer. Its primary application today would be to make sure that all individuals and all groups know and respond to His invitation to spend meaningful time with Him though prayer. No one should feel left out and no one should feel privileged.

People come to a time of corporate prayer from many different emotional and mental locations. Some may be very comfortable and confident in praying out loud. Their personality and background make them unafraid to enter in. Others are very cautious and uncomfortable with even saying (let alone praying) *anything* in a group setting. A key role of the facilitator is to help level the playing field. Applying what Isaiah said in Isaiah 40:4 [Every valley shall be raised up, every mountain and hill made low] how can the one responsible for a time of corporate prayer encourage some to participate a bit more (raise the "valleys") and others to hold back a bit more (lower the "mountains")?

The key here is in the way we give direction. We should seek to make everyone's prayer experience one that would leave them wanting more. We want each person to feel like they contributed to the overall prayer and that they personally interacted in a meaningful way with the Lord.

> *We should seek to make everyone's prayer experience one that would leave them wanting more.*

I remember being with about fifty staff people from a large congregation. We were going to be together for three days. Because this included the entire church staff from their congregation, I knew each of them had a different comfort level concerning their own walk with the Lord and corporate prayer.

In our first session, I referred to Hebrews 4:12, which says, "For the Word of God is alive and powerful…" I made a few comments about how Scripture is active and powerful and how we can receive life from it. Then I asked people to go around the circle and each one share a verse from which they personally had received life or seen God's power. I mentioned that it was an "Open book test" so they could use their Bibles. I knew this was something everyone in the room could do. I encouraged them to just simply share the verse and keep any comments to a minimum.

After each person shared, including myself, I asked them to get with two other people and to use that verse as the basis of a short prayer for the others in their group and for all of us. I gave them an example from my verse, which was Romans 12:1 [Therefore, I urge you, brothers, in view of God's mercy to offer your bodies as living sacrifices…]. In my group I will pray a prayer like, "Father would you please make Dick and Bill more aware of your wonderful mercy and love. Help each of us in this room, over the next couple days, to be more impacted by how you have loved us. Then as a result of that fresh awareness, please let us be more fully surrendered to You and Your ways. Amen."

Because I had given each of them the opportunity to be aware of a key spiritual truth they were personally familiar with, and modeled how they could pray, they launched into their time of prayer with an equal opportunity to pray. Those less inclined to pray were in a smaller group, knew what they could pray and knew they didn't have to pray too long. Those inclined to pray too long and wander knew they had a specific topic and time frame.

In other settings, I have encouraged people to "complete a sentence" in prayer. For example, in one setting we just finished singing the words, "He's altogether lovely, altogether worthy, altogether wonderful to me..." When we finished singing those words, I said something like, "We just sang some wonderful words. Jesus is *altogether* lovely, He is *altogether* worthy, and He is *altogether* wonderful. Now let me ask you a question. What else is He? Let's pray as a group and just tell Him what else He is to us. Begin your prayer with the words, 'Jesus, you are altogether... and then you fill in the words you want to express to Him.'"

As the expression goes, we should put the cookies on the lower shelf. Everyone in the room felt they could participate in that kind of prayer and no one in the room really had the chance to dominate the time of prayer.

➢ **Blessed by Doing** – What is the level of *equal participation* in your prayer group? How can you as a facilitator help balance it so that there is no domination or lack of participation?

United and Ignited

7. Participation – While I am facilitating, what should I be thinking about?

At this point, you have spent time with the Lord in preparation and you may have a sense of where you should begin. The prayer time is underway. Now what? How do you shepherd the flow of this time of prayer so that Jesus is glorified and the participants know they have contributed well to the process?

7.1 How can we direct a dynamic corporate prayer session once it is started?

Let me mention again the importance of hearing the direction of the Holy Spirit in this process. The short (and probably the best) answer to the above question is, "Sense what God is doing and co-operate with Him." It may be good to re-read the answer to Question 3.2 on how the Holy Spirit leads us. More will be said about the role of listening in the next question, but let's address a couple related things at this point.

As you are facilitating a time of prayer, it is essential that you really seek to follow what is taking place. Pay attention to what is going on. This is an added responsibility from simply participating in a time of prayer. As a facilitator you have two responsibilities. You must both participate and lead at the same time.

Scripture combines the responsibility to *watch* and to *pray* on several occasions. I have found it very helpful to have my eyes open as people are praying. I want to observe what is happening. I want to notice expressions. I want to see what kind of responses people are having to what is going on. And sometimes people pray very quietly. I have found that if I look at them when they pray I can catch more of what they are saying than if my eyes are closed.

Let your posture reflect the fact that you are paying attention. It may not be that uncommon for someone to doze off during a time of prayer, but it certainly should not be the facilitator who is catching that nap! There may be times when you will want to lean forward in your chair. There may be times when you will want to kneel or stand. The specific posture is not as important as the fact that it reflects your heart and that you are engaged in what is happening.

➢ **Blessed by Doing** – As you facilitate your prayer group, is your mind and your body fully engaged? Practice intentionally following what is being read, sung, and prayed.

7.2 What is the role of listening in facilitating?

Of all the skills or activities that make corporate prayer meaningful, none is more important than listening. It is essential for both the facilitator and the participants. For prayer to be most effective everyone should be listening to the Holy Spirit, to the prayers being prayed, the songs being sung, and the Scriptures being read. And the participants will go further in prayer as they listen to the instructions of the facilitator.

> *Of all the skills or activities that make corporate prayer meaningful, none is more important than listening.*

We tend to think that prayer is more of a straight, horizontal line from us to another person. We pray for the person over there and it makes a difference. But viewing prayer as the first three legs of the four legs of a "W" is probably a better picture. The best prayers do not begin with us. They begin in the heart of our heavenly Father. He sees a need in a person's life and wants to meet it. He then impresses that need in a pray-ers heart. This is the first leg of the "W" – from Him to us. Then we pray that need back to the Lord. This is the second leg – from us to Him. He then mingles our prayer with His will and moves to meet the need. This is the third leg – from Him to them. All this begins with the heart of God and is triggered by us hearing His desire.

> **Blessed by Doing** – Ask the Lord to increase your desire and capacity to listen to Him and for Him during your times of prayer.

7.2.1 Why is it important to listen... To the Holy Spirit?

The primary purpose of a time of dynamic corporate prayer is that people would encounter God. This is a spiritual activity and requires the action of the Holy Spirit. Jesus said that He is the one who would convince (convict) us of certain spiritual things and then give us what we need to get us from where we are to where He wants us to be. As people come into the presence of the Lord, He then is able to give them what they need, speak to them what needs to be spoken, touch them where they need to be touched, and restore in them what needs to be restored.

We do not accomplish these things, Jesus does through His Spirit. It is not about our plans or abilities, it is His. It is His activity that we need, not our activity. If His will is going to be accomplished, it is essential that we follow His leadership, not seek to impose our leadership upon Him. So, if we want to see His activity take place in prayer it will be because we have heard what He wants to do and cooperated with Him.

As in all forms of ministry, whether it is preaching, teaching, serving, counseling or anything else, to the degree that we think we are the *engine* to make it happen, to that same degree the Lord will let us try. But to the degree that we are convinced we are only a conduit or a tool in the Lord's hand, to that same degree He can use us to accomplish His purposes. This is as true in facilitating prayer as it is in any other area of ministry. What makes a time of corporate prayer dynamic is not our cool idea. It is that somehow we and the pray-ers have caught what the Lord is up to and cooperated with Him. Listening to Him is where this all begins. See also Question 3.2.

➢ **Blessed by Doing** – Repent of times when you have demonstrated the perspective that ministry (prayer ministry and beyond) depends upon your abilities or good ideas. Tell the Lord very clearly that you want to follow His leadership in all ministry circumstances.

7.2.2 Why is it important to listen... To the other pray-ers?

> *What makes a time of corporate prayer dynamic is not our cool idea. It is that somehow we and the pray-ers have caught what the Lord is up to and cooperated with Him.*

As we are facilitating prayer, many times God speaks to us through the prayers of those in the room. When people are submitted to Him, don't bring their own agenda with them, and listen to Him, He will direct their prayers. It is a wise facilitator who listens to the prayers being prayed. Only then does that facilitator have the option of catching how the Lord is leading someone in prayer. I have found this is often the way the Lord leads us in a time of prayer.

On many occasions as I have listened to prayers, there is one prayer that stands out. It is not necessarily because of the volume, or the intensity, or even the content. Other prayers before and after are good, "right on" prayers. But there is something about this prayer that makes it different. You may identify it in many ways. It is anointed, or directed, or more clear, or more passionate. As participants hear that prayer they notice something different about it. As a facilitator hears that prayer, they should recognize it as being different. It is through prayers like this that God often confirms a thought or direction, or begins to redirect to another topic.

> **Blessed by Doing** – Make it your practice to listen to the prayers being prayed in your prayer group. Notice when there is a common thread to them or if there is a prayer that the Lord may use to emphasize a certain direction.

7.2.3 Why is it important to listen... To the songs sung and the Scriptures read?

Just as it is important for the facilitator to listen to the prayers of others, (as mentioned in Question 7.2.2 above) it is also important for them to listen to songs and Scriptures as well. But there is a bit more to mention about songs and Scriptures. The prayers that we hear people pray are always fresh to us. That is, we have not heard that prayer before. The problem with a song or with Scriptures is that we have heard them before, sometimes, many times before. Being over-familiar with a song or a Scripture can rob us of the fresh truth God wants to speak to us from it. So, it is especially important to listen well as these are presented.

I remember a key truth God pointed out to us as someone was reading the prayer of Paul in Ephesians 3. They read verse 14-20. But as they were reading, I especially noticed one particular word in verse 18 – "...may have power, together with all the saints, to grasp how wide and long and high and deep is the love of Christ." I have heard and prayed that verse on many occasions. It has wonderful things to say and pray about His great love!

But this time, as I was listening to it being read, I noticed the word "together." Paul's prayer was that a fuller understanding of love would come to a group. There was something about each person responding, receiving, and interacting with His love that would affect the other people and their ability to grasp His love. So, when he finished reading and praying through that passage, I pointed out that word and gave a very brief explanation. I invited the pray-ers to go back to that passage and consider and pray from the significance of the word "together." As we prayed it was confirmed on several occasions that this was a truth the Lord wanted us to grasp and pray at that time.

On another occasion we had just sung the song, "Come, Now is the Time to Worship." One of the lines encourages us to come, "just as you are to worship." It struck me that we were coming to Him in many different conditions. So, I invited us to sing the song again considering the phrase, "just as you are" with the anticipation that we would share how we "are" when we completed the song. After we sang, I briefly restated my invitation encouraging them to begin their prayers with the words, "Jesus, right now I am _____" (for example, "excited" or "discouraged" or "tired" or "resting.")

For several minutes we expressed to God our "just-as-you-are" condition. This helped people evaluate and understand their current condition. People began to pray deep prayers reflecting their real condition. We worship more authentically and got to know each other more.

These times of prayer were possible, not because I had a thought-through agenda, but because I was listening to what was happening, interacted with the Lord about how we could pray what He pointed out, and invited people into it. In each of these cases, the prayers were much higher and deeper than they would have been had I come up with a nice idea of my own. See also Question 4.1.

➢ **Blessed by Doing** – When a song is sung or a Scripture is read, lean forward in your thinking, especially when it is familiar to you. See if the Lord highlights a specific thought that could establish an entry point for prayer.

7.2.4 Why is it important to listen… To the facilitator?

The topics of prayer in most times of corporate prayer are not necessarily related to each other. As I mentioned before, it is more like individual prayer in a group setting. Each person prays what is on their heart with little or no direction from a facilitator and the prayers seldom flow with each other. But when there is some direction, some instruction, some suggestion, some facilitation of prayer, the prayers can not only relate to each other, but they can augment each other. The prayer experience for the pray-er and the impact of the prayer can be much more significant.

But this is dependent upon the facilitator giving clear direction and also upon the pray-ers hearing and following that direction. Just as a symphony, orchestra, or choir needs to follow the director in order to move together and produce good music, so also a group of pray-ers greatly benefits from having a person who *conducts* a time of prayer. As a reminder here, it is vitally important that the facilitator seek to be sensitive to the Lord so he or she has a confidence they are moving in the direction and at the pace the Holy Spirit is moving.

It is also the responsibility of the facilitator to graciously communicate this value (following the directives of the facilitator) to the pray-ers. Here are some ways that I have done this.

Often I will begin a time of prayer by acting as though I know they want to and will follow me. By that I mean I give clear directions as though it is our normal practice. I give some explanation about what we have done and why we have done it after we have prayed for a while. I refer to this as the "show and tell" method. We do the instruction before we talk about it.

> *... so also a group of pray-ers greatly benefits from having a person who* conducts *a time of prayer.*

If you are in a setting where some of the people are familiar with dynamic corporate prayer, you can ask the group to review a few key things that can make the time be most productive.

Ask two or three people beforehand to share what their understanding of how this prayer experience could be different than other prayer experiences. In the process encourage them to emphasize the value of listening to and following suggestions.

It is possible for the facilitator to communicate this and a few other key thoughts toward the beginning of a time of prayer in a manner that is not like passing out the rules of prayer.

However it is accomplished, you will find that corporate prayer becomes far better when people are on the same page. Listening to the Holy Spirit, to the prayers of the people, to the songs and the Scriptures read as well as to the facilitator will help everyone get there.

➤ **Blessed by Doing** – As you facilitate, be succinct in your directions. Find creative, brief ways to encourage the pray-ers in your group to listen and follow the directions you offer them.

7.3 What role does creativity play in facilitating dynamic corporate prayer?

• There are about 25 pastors in the room for a morning of prayer. To begin the time of prayer I ask them to gather in groups of three. I ask them to select one of the, "fruit of the Spirit" they would like to grow in. Then I ask them to pray that that fruit would be more evident in the lives of the two other people in their group.

• There was a feud between two denominations in a city. "Every-one knows about it." At the communion table that evening the facilitator had representatives from the two denominations stand over the communion table and conduct a funeral for the feud.

• There were nearly 80 people together enjoying Jesus in worship and prayer. We had a time of proclaiming some of Jesus' Bib-lical names. Soon I encouraged them to continue on pro-claiming more names of Jesus but they, "Couldn't use any more Biblical names. You have to describe who He is to you in modern terms without referencing Scripture."

• As we were approaching communion, the facilitator asked peop-le to not only come to the table and receive, but to also give Jesus something. "Present to Jesus something you have in your possession right now and tell Him why you are giving that to Him." Name tags, wallets, keys, pictures, smart phones, shoes, change, and many other items were laid on the table before the pastors receive the communion elements.

- As the session of prayer was nearly over, the facilitator gathered everyone around the communion table in the middle of the room. He encouraged people to pray a one-word prayer of thanks to the Lord for what they had just experienced. The time of prayer continued word by word for close to five minutes.
- After singing "At the Cross... Where I first saw the light..." I pointed to pastors one after another and asked, "Where did you first see the light?" The first few responses set the stage for a deep time of rejoicing in His salvation. "In my apartment while trying to get high." "In jail as a stranger came to talk about Jesus with anyone who would listen." "Just before I was going to go commit a crime."

Each of these prayer activities expresses not so much the creativity of the facilitator as much as it does the creativity of God. God is infinitely creative. His creativity today is no less then it was when He first said, "Let there be light." And when we let Him, His creativity can flow through us and affect our times of prayer.

Creativity in prayer is a key component in helping ordinary prayer become dynamic prayer. But it is not our creativity, it is His. He knows the specific needs, personalities, desires, history, quirks, and passions of the people in the room at that moment. We don't. He knows what needs to be done. We don't. So, as we listen to the Lord, often times, He will lead us to do something that is out of the ordinary.

We should not seek creativity just to be creative. But we should not rule out something we have never done before just because it might stretch us or because we aren't sure where that specific step may take us. Facilitating dynamic corporate prayer is often a journey where you aren't certain of all the turns you will make. This is where it is very helpful to have a person you can check with during the time of prayer. Confirmation from someone else helps us move with greater confidence. And a caution from someone else can save us from a lot of trouble. But, we may miss it at times! If you try something that doesn't work, don't try to force it to work. Hit the eject button and move on.

A person does not need to be known as a creative person before they can be a good facilitator, but as they are open to the creativity of the Holy Spirit, they will be able to lead prayer times that are more dynamic.

➢ **Blessed by Doing** – Tell the Lord you are open to new fresh ways to facilitate corporate prayer. Ask Him to let you catch His creativity. Then, in appropriate ways, risk. If you sense the Holy Spirit asking you to do something you have never done before, gently, but directly, encourage the group to do it.

7.4 What is the role of *prayer tracks* in dynamic corporate prayer?

There are times when it is helpful to present a *prayer track* to assist the flow of prayer. A prayer track is a specific question to be answered or a sentence to be completed in prayer that can bring greater focus to a time of corporate prayer. As I referenced earlier, this can be a great way to help equalize a time of prayer. These work best when they are spontaneously connected to what just happened.

Here are some specific guidelines.
- Listen with fresh ears to what is being said or sung.
- Notice any line that the Lord seems to highlight to you.
- Ask Him how that idea could be turned into a prayer.
- Give succinct directions to the group and possibly give an example.
- These should be in the form of a prayer stated directly to the Lord, rather than simply a comment about Him.
- It is best when these allow people to be specific in their prayers.
- It is helpful to (at times) encourage a corporate response.

For example immediately following a very meaningful time of prayer about God's grace, it may be appropriate to encourage a group to, "Express to the Lord a specific time when you know you sensed God's amazing grace. Please begin your prayer with the words, 'God I know I experienced Your amazing grace when....' and then you complete it from there." A possible corporate response following each prayer would be, "Yes, your grace is amazing!"

This type of prayer activity can be very helpful, but, we should not get caught up in them and let the activity override the primary purpose of the time of prayer. It would be very unusual for this to be a steady diet. Prayer introduced by a prayer track can be very meaningful in and of itself, and it can help lead a group to times of very deep prayer. Also, we would not want the brief prayer encouraged by this style of prayer keep a group from entering into times of more extended prayer.

> **Blessed by Doing** – Read over the guidelines above several times until you are quite familiar with them. Then ask the Lord to show you opportunities to provide a *track* for people to pray upon.

7.5 What are the signals of a change in topic and how can I navigate that change?

My father worked as a railway mail carrier for over 20 years until they discontinued the service in the 1960's. Since he knew it was going to be discontinued, he smuggled me on a trip when I was in the sixth grade. Riding from Seattle to Spokane and back in a mail car was a great childhood experience. There was only one mail car on the train. The others contained some kind of freight. What held each of the cars together were couplers. A coupler is the small connecting point between two train cars, each carrying important but different products.

God has many cars on His prayer train. What holds them together properly are the coupling points. In a time of prayer, it is important for the facilitator to notice and navigate those points. We may stay on one topic for a short period of time or for a few hours. What makes it a smooth ride is to recognize God's transition point and flow with it.

In a multi-hour or multi-day prayer time, the most natural transition points come related to a break. Different factors I try to read that help determine when we should take a break are...

- The size and the maturity level of the group – generally speaking, the larger the group and the more mature the group, the longer a session can go and still maintain spiritual vitality. If it is a smaller group or a group not that comfortable in corporate prayer, you will want to make the sessions shorter.

- The level of engagement of the pray-ers – if the pray-ers are still engaged (with prayers, songs and Scriptures) continue on. If they are beginning to become disengaged, consider a break or a change in direction. If people are squirming, yawning, or sleeping, you missed it, it is a bit past time for a break!

- The time of day – afternoon, especially right after lunch, our bodies are more concerned with physical digestion than spiritual digestion. These sessions may be more effective if they are either shorter, spent in small groups, or spent in a different setting.

- If you sense the Lord is leading you to a different topic that should/could warrant a longer prayer time, it would not be best to engage in that just before you should be taking a break.

Other signals for a change of focus (in either a longer or shorter time of prayer) are similar to what has been written earlier regarding sensing the leading of the Holy Spirit (see Question 3.2). A more weighty prayer or song, a highlighted idea in a song or Scripture, a lingering thought from a previous song or prayer, or a very clear thought based upon what is being prayed right now. Each of these can be a cue that God is turning a corner or making a shift. When you notice one of these things, be aware, interact with God about them, talk with your co-facilitator, and anticipate some confirmation.

If the group is praying on a specific topic, there is generally a time when it becomes clear that you have covered what the Lord wanted prayed at that point. This sense of completeness is also a cue for a corner.

When we allow the Holy Spirit to make these transitions, they are wonderfully smooth and relate well to each other. But it is also helpful to remember that often times it seems we recognize these transitions in the rear-view mirror. If we keep our eyes "fixed on Jesus" He is able to navigate us through these transitions.

An interesting observation I have made is that when someone in the prayer group tries to lead the group into a different focus or topic, when one of the participants seeks to turn a prayer corner or moves into praying their own agenda rather than the one the Lord has put us on, it seldom goes well. There are many appropriate topics of prayer at any given moment. There are always missionaries to be prayed for, wars we desire to end, children in need, physical needs to be addressed, etc. But when someone begins to pray on a different and completely unrelated topic, it rarely leads to a smooth transition. See Question 7.6 below for help if this happens.

> *When we allow the Holy Spirit to make these transitions, they are wonderfully smooth and relate well to each other.*

The greatest assurance that the transitions will be smooth is to encourage everyone to try to be sensitive to the Holy Spirit, to listen to the prayers of the others, and to have their prayers relate to the previous prayer and/or the topic. With some simple instruction and clear facilitation, transitions can go very well and topics can build upon each other.

➤ **Blessed by Doing** – As you facilitate longer times of prayer, anticipate times of re-direction. Ask the Lord to make you sensitive to them.

7.6 How can we get back on track if we get side-tracked?

When someone does begin praying in a different direction, the facilitator has two responsibilities: to protect the integrity of the direction God has put us on and to protect the integrity of the individual(s) involved. Both responsibilities must be held in balance.

The second responsibility is fulfilled to the degree we speak with grace. We don't want to dishonor someone because they have prayed what might be considered a wrong prayer at the wrong time, but we also don't want them to continue to pray in a direction the group is not going at the time. The first responsibility should be fulfilled in stages.

Most of the time this can be done with the help of either a prayer, a song, or a Scripture. I will often invite a few other people who are experienced in dynamic corporate prayer to be on the point for this kind of thing and help me get it back on track. This way the facilitator is not the one who is doing all the correction.

If, for example, the group is praying on the theme of the greatness of God and someone prays a prayer about their wayward son (and it is clearly not related to God's greatness) then either the facilitator or one of the people he/she has asked to help could pray the group back on track or begin singing a song such as "How Great is our God" or read a Scripture such as, a few verses from Isaiah 40. In this way, the person who prayed for their child does not feel like they have been corrected, and the theme can continue.

If the same person continues to pray on topics unrelated to where the rest of the group is praying, then it may be necessary to speak with them in private. As an outside facilitator, I have found the best way to approach this is to get confirmation of your thoughts from a couple people who know the person well, then go together and encourage them to listen a bit more before they pray.

There are two questions I have encouraged people to ask when they have some thoughts which may lead to a prayer. 1) Is this idea for me, or is it for the group? That is, does this topic relate only to me? Or is it something the group could relate to as well? And 2) is this for now or is it for later? That is, does it fit with what the Lord is doing right now? These are questions you may want to mention

> *Two key questions: Now or later? For me or the group?*

toward the beginning of your time of prayer, and if you need to talk to someone privately you could encourage them to ask these questions before they begin to pray out loud.

> ➢ **Blessed by Doing** – First of all, as you facilitate, give clear directions. Also train others you trust to help you notice when the group may be getting off track and encourage them to pray, sing, or read the group back on track. Finally, as you feel it is appropriate, encourage the pray-ers in your group to ask the two questions mentioned above.

7.7 How does facilitating a large group differ from facilitating smaller groups?

I have been asked about the "ideal group size" for a time of corporate prayer. My answer is that any size group can be led in dynamic corporate prayer if their hearts are ready and if the facilitator will lead them well. I have facilitated small groups of 4 or 5 and groups of several hundred. The issue is not the size of the group, but in the way it is facilitated. The basic principles are the same but the specific application of those principles should be altered to fit the situation.

Here, in chart form, are some values and considerations contrasting larger and smaller groups.

United and Ignited

Value

Larger group	Smaller group
Greater number of possible pray-ers can lead to more energy in prayer.	Smaller number of pray-ers can lead to more people praying.
The dynamic of strength and volume of worship.	The dynamic of quietness and intimacy.

Facilitation considerations

Instructions must be brief and specific.	Instructions can be more general and flexible.
Facilitator must speak in such a way so as to command the attention of the group.	Can be more relaxed and interactive.
The sessions can be generally longer.	The sessions should be shorter.
The length of time on a given topic or prayer activity can be longer.	The length of time on a give topic or activity should be shorter.
Should encourage succinct prayers. Long prayers are damaging to large prayer groups.	Individual prayers can be somewhat longer.
Should make use of smaller groups of 3-6 at times.	Breaking into smaller groups is not as important.
May need to use a sound system. If so, it is necessary to think through how microphones are used.	No electronic amplification needed.

I have found that a group of between 30 and 50 people is my favorite size. This is a group small enough that no electronics are needed and we can get to know each other fairly quickly. Yet it is large enough to have good energy for worship or a topic of prayer. From this size group you can also break into several smaller groups.

➤ **Blessed by Doing** – Consider, appreciate, and apply the benefits of the size of the group you are facilitating.

120

8. Evaluation – What should I consider and process after a time of corporate prayer?

When your time of prayer is over, the responsibility of the facilitator is not yet over. If you simply say, "Amen" pick up your Bible and go on your way, you will miss some very important responsibilities of facilitating dynamic corporate prayer.

One of the things I do regularly after the time of prayer has concluded is pray for the people who were in attendance. In Philippians 1:6 God says He will complete what He begins. In a time of corporate prayer God will often begin certain things. It is very appropriate that we keep on praying that the things He began in people's lives, known and unknown, would be completed.

> **Blessed by Doing** – Make it your practice to pray for the time of prayer as soon as possible after it is finished.

8.1 Apart from the actual time of prayer, how can I train myself to facilitator better?

If we consider facilitating corporate prayer a valuable ministry, we will want to continually improve our facilitation skills. We will pray that the Lord will keep us close to Him and grow our level of sensitivity to Him. We will seek to increase our confidence in hearing His voice. In addition to these things there are some specific things we can do to grow.

I try to relate most of what I hear and experience to corporate prayer. (See also Question 6.4.) I have made it a habit that when I listen to a sermon I ask myself, "If I were preaching this sermon, how would I encourage the congregation to be praying?" When I hear a song, I think of how we might be able to pray from a certain line or idea from it. And when I read or hear Scripture, I consider how this text or truth might be used to lead a group in prayer. Thoughts and ideas for facilitating dynamic corporate prayer have come to me from things I have seen on the internet, conversations with others, and magazine articles. If we intentionally think about it, we will see many opportunities to grow in these skills.

This practice may seem unusual, but I would encourage each person who has any influence over the spiritual welfare of others to try this and see if it does not give you more and greater ability to accomplish this God-given calling. One of the reasons our prayers reach to the lowest common denominator is because we do not *think* about how we can pray better.

Since practice makes perfect, look for times to facilitate any group in corporate prayer. You could incorporate these principles into an existing accountability or home group. Or you could recruit a few friends for a "six week experiment." If you're a parent, you have a built-in opportunity. (More on this topic in Section 11.)

> *One of the reasons our prayers reach to the lowest common denominator is because we do not think about how we can pray better.*

Finally, talk to others and glean from their experience. When I learned to play the guitar I took very few lessons. Most of what I learned came from watching someone who was better than me and then bugging them to teach me some of what I saw them do. If you want to grow in facilitating corporate prayer, use the same process. You can even learn from people who are not experienced in it. You can ask friends about what makes corporate prayer most meaningful. If you are a pastor, ask another pastor about what he has learned to really engage people in prayer. If you are a parent, ask another parent. You can learn even from the seemingly negative answers.

The bottom line is that if you really want to improve your ability to facilitate dynamic corporate prayer, you will find ways to learn and you will improve. And the Holy Spirit will help you.

> **Blessed by Doing** – Regularly ask yourself if you are growing in your ability to facilitate corporate prayer. Ask others about what was good and not-so-good about their prayer experiences. Consider these ideas and learn from them.

8.2 How can I evaluate the effectiveness of a given session of prayer?

I do not want to encourage introspection, but I do want to encourage evaluation. If we don't evaluate, we don't grow. Here are things I look for when I am evaluating a time of prayer.

- What was the level of group engagement? Were there long gaps or was there a lot of participation? Even though silence can be a very meaningful time, there are other times when silence can mean people are not engaged.

- Did most everyone pray or did some dominate and others go dormant?

- What was the depth of the prayers? Often, as people really encounter God, the tears flow freely. This is not the only evidence, but it is an evidence of being deeply touched by God. In fact, it would be good to have a few boxes of "ministry towellets" (tissues) available at times.

- What was the *spirit* of the group before and after the time of prayer? Connecting with others and Jesus in prayer generally brings great refreshment. Other times there is a great sense of conviction and repentance. Asking for input from the leaders of the group, what they were sensing, can be very helpful.

- Were there times when the presence of the Lord was very obvious in the room? This may seem like a subjective question, but when you have encountered God with others through prayer, you know that sense of peace, refreshment, clarity, edification, and encouragement that goes with it.

- Can you look back and see specific ways the Lord set up and led themes and topics of prayer? I have been in sessions of prayer when two people began singing the same song at the same time in the same key. Also, I have heard people begin reading the same verses of Scripture at the same time. These and other forms of confirmation give you assurance of His leading.
- Did we pray much from the Scriptures? I have found this to be a good standard to go by.
- Was the worship far more than just singing? Was it engaging and did it flow together with prayer and Scripture? Some of the deepest times of worship are when we begin singing a song, but get stuck on a specific aspect of it and linger there for a period of time, praying and reading and then singing some more.
- When we prayed for certain requests, were did they fit with what was happening or did they seem like an intrusion?

In the long run, the best way to evaluate the effectiveness of dynamic corporate prayer is in the testimony of changed lives. As people develop a deeper love for the Savior, you know you are investing well.

➢ **Blessed by Doing** – Regularly evaluate times of corporate prayer whether you facilitate them or not. Don't become critical, but do become critique-al. Use the bullet points above as a guide.

8.3 How can I help pray-ers (in my group or congregation) continue to grow in dynamic corporate pray-er?

If you get to pray with the same group of people on an ongoing basis, in a home group, a congregation, or a family, you have the possibility of seeing some great, long-term results. An ongoing diet of Spirit-led, worship-fed, Scripture-based, corporate prayer will produce results that cannot happen in just a session or two. In this setting, the goal should be not just to help the people in the room pray more and better, but also to equip them to pass on to others the things they have learned from you.

This can happen in three different ways. First, while you are together, you can assist them grow in their capacity to notice the activity of the Holy Spirit. You can also help them learn how to take what they have learned in the group and practice it in their own lives. And finally, you can encourage them to make and take opportunities to facilitate prayer in other groups.

At times as you facilitate, talk about why you have done what you did. You can give them opportunity to ask questions. You can ask them questions as well. Do some "show and tell" with them. Lead them in some dynamic corporate prayer, then talk about what they experienced and why you directed them as you did. In this way you can grow and discover more about corporate prayer together.

You can give them some suggestions as to how to pray throughout the week. Together, your home group could meditate and pray through a chapter of Scripture. Then, when you gather together you can do together what you have been doing in-dividually. Or a family could think through some agreed upon *concordance praying* Scriptures on a topic for a couple days, then spend 15-20 minutes after a meal some evening praying together from some of those Scriptures. (See Question 5.3.)

Asking a couple simple questions will help with this. Such as, "How can I help the people in my group not only pray more effectively here, but also when they are alone? Or, how can I help them help others to continue in this type of prayer?" As you ask these and other question like them, you will be surprised at how many ideas you (and the Lord) will come up with.

> *Lead them in some dynamic corporate prayer, then talk about what they experienced and why you directed them as you did.*

➤ **Blessed by Doing** – Regularly consider how you can encourage the people in your prayer group to continue to pray more and better prayers in other settings.

9. Congregations, Part I – How can dynamic corporate prayer be incorporated into the life of a congregation?

After encouraging a pastor friend to incorporate more dynamic corporate prayer into their Sunday morning worship service, he took some initial steps. While introducing a time of prayer during a Sunday morning service, he quipped, "Some of you may be thinking, 'Now you've gone and done it, pastor. You're trying to bring prayer right into the middle of our church service!'"

Even though he was completely jesting, sometimes it seems like encouraging people to pray out loud during a church service is simply going too far! Many times our Sunday service has become a very passive experience. The idea of seeing our weekend service as a primary opportunity to help disciple people into a more meaning prayer life is either not noticed or ruled out. If we take any steps to encourage prayer, it is generally preaching about prayer or modeling prayer rather than actually praying. This does not have to be the case.

Much of our efforts have been to encourage people to come to a special time of prayer. We should not stop this, but the truth is many people who attend a weekend service will never come to an announced prayer meeting. So, instead of trying to move the people to prayer, why not move prayer to the people?

> ➤ **Blessed by Doing** – Consider how you can make prayer a more integral part of what is already taking place in your congregation or ministry. Instead of having other times of prayer, bring more prayer to what is already there.

Instead of trying to move the people to prayer, why not move prayer to the people?

9.1 What is the role of the senior leader in developing dynamic corporate prayer in a congregation?

Our ability to influence does not go beyond our ability to influence. That is, we can only influence those within our sphere of influence. Dynamic corporate prayer will influence a congregation only to the degree the Senior Pastor is involved in the process. The ultimate responsibility of a congregation being devoted to prayer or becoming a house of prayer cannot be delegated or assigned to someone else. Parts of it can be, but ultimately, the main preaching pastor is the one who determines the value of this aspect of discipleship. He determines this by his public statements and his private behavior.

Biblically, the responsibility for prayer is not like other responsibilities. The one who is responsible for the ministry of the Word is also charged with being devoted to prayer (see Acts 6:4, 1 Timothy 2:1-2, etc.). And practically, I have not seen a congregation be strong in prayer without this.

> *Biblically, the responsibility for prayer is not like other responsibilities.*

It is not true, though, that the Senior Pastor must be responsible to do everything necessary to have this happen in his congregation. He should seek to develop people around him who also have a heart for prayer and will team with him in the process. But without a heart for prayer in general, and dynamic corporate prayer in particular, it will always be less than it could be.

➤ **Blessed by Doing** – For Senior Pastors – honestly consider your commitment to have dynamic corporate prayer be an integral part of your congregation. The 6:4 Fellowship is a great tool to help a Senior Pastor who wants to move forward in this area. www.64fellowship.org.

> **Blessed by Doing** – For those who are not Senior Pastors – consider what your appropriate role should be in helping this happen in your congregation. Honor your pastor and your congregational leadership! Work with them, not around them.

9.2 What is the role of dynamic corporate prayer in a weekend service?

I understand the value of being sensitive to those who may not feel comfortable praying out loud, especially because they are visiting or new in their faith. And I am realistic that the size of a congregation determines much of what can be accomplished. But what does it say about our priorities when a person has become a follower of Jesus and has been a regular part of a congregation for 6 months, a year, or longer, and they still feel very uncomfortable about praying out loud? We will see more mature believers if we train them in corporate prayer.

Whether it is spoken or unspoken, the clear rule of most congregations is, "If it is important, it happens during our weekend service." This is the primary time when the people gather. And this is the time when our values are most obvious. Although it is not the only time, it can be a vitally important time to assist people in this valuable discipline. So, why not make good use of this time to equip people in corporate prayer? You may be asking, "Is it possible to help train the established believer without scaring off the brand-new visitor?" My answer is a resounding, "Yes."

So, even though corporate prayer can and should be practiced at other times and other places in addition to the main weekend service, we will accomplish the goal of seeing more people enter into more meaningful prayer if we make use of the primary gathering as well as other times.

> **Blessed by Doing** – Think of 2 or 3 fresh ways corporate prayer could take place in your primary weekend services.

9.2.1 How can it relate to our preaching and teaching?

I am not advocating that corporate prayer be a separate part of our services. I am advocating it becomes a natural part of them. That we would incorporate it into all we do in our services. How can this happen? It could be part of a time of welcoming people. It could be part of the announcements. It certainly should be part of the worship experience. (More in Question 9.2.2 below.) And it can be a regular part of our preaching/teaching.

I have challenged pastors to "tithe their preaching/teaching to prayer." What do I mean by that? First, that about 10% of the Sunday morning messages be on the topic of prayer. This could be one message out of ten, or it could be a portion of several messages. But if prayer is a vital aspect of a disciple's life, it seems it deserves at least this much emphasis. Second, that about 10% of the sermon preparation be given to prayer. If a pastor normally spends (for example) 10 hours preparing their message, why not spend 9 hours in preparation and one hour in prayer related to that message? Finally, if they normally preach or teach for 30 minutes, why not preach or teach for 27 minutes and devote the other 3 minutes to corporate prayer. This plan can be followed not only by pastors but also by Sunday School teachers, home group leaders, and anyone who presents the Word publically.

> *I have challenged pastors to "tithe their preaching/teaching to prayer."*

During the time of prayer as they are preparing, they would pray in three ways. First, they would pray through the content of their message. They would pray that God would align their words with His Word so His Spirit can communicate it to His people. They would pray it through, point by point, asking God to engraft that portion of His Word into the lives of those who hear. This is a great practical demonstration that we are not depending upon our words or abilities, but upon God and His ability to communicate His Word through us. And obviously, it gives God an opportunity to energize the ideas He has given us.

During this time of prayer, they would also consider how the hearers could or should be praying individually because of this message. We regularly ask how people can live differently because of a message preached. Why not also ask how they can pray differently?

Finally, they would ask God how He wants the people to be engaged in corporate prayer, based upon the content of the message. Then, the preacher/teacher would facilitate a time of corporate prayer. The way this may work in your setting is dependent upon many variables, but it can be done in any setting. The goal is to give as many people as possible the best opportunity to encounter God through prayer. Let it be led by His Spirit, directed to Jesus in worship, based upon Scripture with an opportunity for as many people as possible to participate.

Just as a pastor does not determine the content of his message based upon the comfort level of his congregation, so also, if a pastor understands that part of his discipling responsibilities is to teach everyone in his congregation to pray, he will not let the comfort level of his congregation determine if he helps them grow in this area. In the long run, we will get what we value. If we value teaching people to pray, we will take simple, consistent, steps to help them get there.

Here are some things to consider.

- The prayer could be all at one time or it could be in 2 or 3 smaller blocks.
- It could take place at the end, the beginning, or even during the message.
- It should be directly related to the message being shared.
- Giving them some kind of visual is helpful. For example use a slide on a screen, a bookmark, or include it on regular sermon notes. A card or bookmark with a verse or key idea on it would allow them to pray right then as well as take it with them as a reminder throughout the week.

- It should not be the same format each week. Tap into the Holy Spirit's creativity.

Here are some suggested ways to structure or format a prayer time.
- Using small groups
  o "Please turn and get with 3 or 4 other people (or a larger group at times) right where you are. Make sure you include someone you don't know or don't know very well."
  o "If you are with your family, get with them this morning. If you are not with your family, turn and form a 'temporary prayer family.'"
  o "Please move around a bit and form groups of men and women. Make sure you include different ages in your group."
  o If there are three things to pray about, ask them to get in groups of three and each one in the group decide beforehand which item they will pray about.
- Have different groups of people pray.
  o "This morning, let's just have people under 18 years old (or you pick the number) do the praying."
  o Let's have only the men (or women) pray in your group this time.
  o Ask people to pray for the person on their right (or left).
  o Ask people to pray in, "a conversational volume" all at the same time.
- Before you begin sharing, project a key verse from your message on a screen. Invite the people to read it over a few times and "find a prayer" within that verse. Then, after a few seconds, invite them to join with 2 or 3 others and pray that prayer.
- At the end of a message have two or three people prepared to pray some of the key ideas from the message.
- After you finish a key point during your message, invite a person (this could be spontaneous or planned) to pray a brief

prayer that the Lord would help each person in the congregation not only understand and remember this point, but to live it throughout the week.

Here are some key things to remember when you will be asking people to pray in a small group during a Sunday Service.

- The main reason people are afraid to pray out loud is because they don't know what to say. They are afraid they will feel embarrassed or inadequate. They are afraid of saying a dumb thing or praying a prayer that may be considered wrong.

- You can address this concern by helping them find a way to pray. You can give them some specific options. This will help them gain confidence.

- Give them a little time to think about how they can pray and even some suggested wording. Perhaps share a brief example of how they could pray.

- Give directions that are easy enough that anyone in the room could follow them. Simplicity is better than complexity. Encourage everyone to pray a brief, meaningful, simple prayer.

- I would add a caution here, when we ask people to get into small groups. If you give people time to talk before they pray (rather than just to think) they will tend to talk and not get to prayer. I don't think it is necessary to have a time to introduce oneself or chat before the time of prayer.

- I have found approaching this time light-heartedly is better than approaching it very seriously. I know that prayer is a serious thing, but if we make it *grave* it will seem like it belongs in a cemetery! If you can move people from laughter to prayer, it will set them more at ease.

- If you are just starting to do this with your group, I would not recommend a lengthy explanation and justification. Perhaps a brief statement about doing something a little different followed by brief instructions with the full expectation that this is a normal thing to do.

- You want to always give people the option not to pray out loud. You want to encourage them to stretch their present experience, but you don't want to force anyone to participate. Saying something like, "If you just don't feel comfortable praying out loud at this point, that is fine. But we do want you to know that this is a safe place. And it would be great if you could reflect back on this morning as the first time you ever prayed out loud."

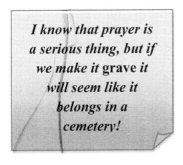

I know that prayer is a serious thing, but if we make it **grave** *it will seem like it belongs in a cemetery!*

- Remember that most people come to church because they desire a closer relationship with the Lord. They know that prayer is a key part of how that happens. If you sense resistance, it may be simply because this is a *new* activity, not because it is a *prayer* activity.
- If this is a value to your congregation, it can become the new normal over a period of time. Stick with it and you will see good results.

The details of how you lead your group in prayer are not as important as the process of asking the Lord how He wants the prayer time to happen. Just as it is very right that the preacher/teacher gives themselves to the preparation of the Word, so also it is right for them to give themselves to prayer. (See Acts 6:4).

➢ **Blessed by Doing** – When you are committed to implement dynamic corporate prayer as part of your primary weekend services, select three suggestions I have made in the answer above about how prayer can be incorporated into your preaching/teaching time. Prioritize them. Do some Holy Spirit customization on them to fit your congregation. Try them.

9.2.2 How can it relate to our worship?

We know that worship is more than music. But sometimes the only intentional expression of worship in our services is through music. What if we had a worship service and used no music whatsoever? What if we enhanced the time of worship through music with a time of worship through prayer? Or what if it was a regular practice to allow for some corporate prayer based upon the words to some of the songs we are singing?

The specifics I have mentioned in the previous question as well as all of the questions in Section 4 and also Question 7.4 can be applied here. It could look like the following: As you are singing a song, the worship leader could pause for a minute and point out the power of the words the congregation just sang. Then he/she could invite them to ponder them a bit and get in groups and pray.

If you sing a song about God's majesty, you could have a time when people complete the sentence, "God I have seen your majesty in _____." There are countless other topics similar to this.

A worship leader could have people read a verse on the screen together, then give a, "One word prayer" based upon something in that verse. This can happen in a large group setting as well as a smaller group setting.

You could write a prayer that would be read/prayed by various groups in the congregation. The men could read one part and the women another. Or one person could read a portion and the group respond.

Some of these things take planning, and that is a very valid way to lead corporate prayer. But when it is spontaneously directed by the Lord, it can also be very meaningful. It feels a bit more risky, but it can also produce some very meaningful ministry and worship times. A key to making this possible is for the worship leader to be thinking about the content of what is being sung more than the logistics of the music being played. If they have their mind and heart set on the Lord and what is being sung about Him, their hearts and minds can be touched and the Holy Spirit can help them lead the congregation in creative, dynamic prayer. If their primary focus is on the music, they may miss many opportunities the Lord may set up to have people really encounter Him.

> *A key to making this possible is for the worship leader to be thinking about the content of what is being sung more than the logistics of the music being played.*

It would also be very helpful if the worship leader practiced what I mentioned in Question 6.2 and 6.3 on preparing one's heart to lead corporate prayer.

➢ **Blessed by Doing** – As you plan the worship service, consider two or three ways corporate prayer could be incorporated into the worship portion of your service and try one.

9.2.3 How can it relate to the pastoral prayer?

Many, if not most congregations have a specific time in their service when the pastor prays for specific needs, the message, people in need, etc. Are there things the pray-er can do to help others who are not verbally praying engage as much as possible? Here are some ideas.

- Before the prayer, share a couple brief, but specific things about what or who will be prayed for so the people have enough background to identify with what is being prayed.
- Project a slide with a list of four prayer items. Explain that you will pray for the first one and the last one and ask them to select one of the middle two to pray for silently.
- Ask people to gather in groups of 3 or 4. Explain that when you mention a topic, you will pause. During that pause you would like one person to pray a brief prayer for the person or topic mentioned. You will then continue on in your prayer to the next topic.
- Have part of your prayer be repetitive. Ask the people to repeat, phrase by phrase, the prayer you are praying. This can work

very well if the pray-er prays with confidence and leads in a brief, thought-through prayer.

- Relate the requests to a specific verse. Read (or project) that verse, then pray for the request based upon the verse.
- It can work well to write out a prayer that can be projected and read together. Some of it can be read by the leader and some by the congregation.
- Having a different person pray for each request can also help the people follow along.

The main point is that if we ask the Lord how He wants that prayer time to go, and we follow His leadership, we will not get stuck doing it the way we always do it. Brevity and creativity are not virtues in and of themselves, but neither are lengthy prayers prayed in the same way each week without fresh consideration.

➢ **Blessed by Doing** – Ask the Lord how corporate prayer can or should be incorporated into the pastoral prayer so that more people are able to participate more fully.

9.3 How can it make a difference in home groups or Sunday School classes?

What is the best environment to learn and grow in corporate prayer? Generally, it is a group of people who meet together regularly, who know each other, who study the Word together, and who want to grow in Christ together. All these components make a smaller group setting one of the best places for people to experience and grow in dynamic corporate prayer.

Unfortunately, when prayer is a part of a small group, we tend to move to the *lowest* common denominator of asking for prayer requests ("What are your prayer requests?") and making sure each request is covered ("Who will pray for _____?"). We tend to get to this point because that is what we have been exposed to, and we don't give time, thought, or prayer into how to do it differently. But there is so much more we can do!

If the leader of the group will take the challenge to "tithe the teaching to prayer" (see Question 9.1) there can be great progress made. Except in this setting (as opposed to a Weekend Service) there can be more than a couple minutes given to prayer.

Instead of our prayer being unrelated to what we have (or will) study in our meeting, why not shape our prayers directly around the study? We could use a Scripture or series of Scriptures on a specific theme and, using some of what was written in Section 5, base our prayers on that theme. It is not wrong to give people an opportunity to mention specific requests, but why not relate the way we pray about that request to the topic we have been studying? This may not always be possible, but it is always good to see if that is an option.

> *It is not wrong to give people an opportunity to mention specific requests, but why not relate the way we pray about that request to the topic we have been studying?*

Another thing that will make corporate prayer more dynamic is to not always pray at the same time in the meeting. Instead of having an opening prayer and later on the main block of prayer, why not mix it up? Having the primary time of prayer before the main teaching is a great way to set up the teaching. Or teach for a bit, then having brief prayer responses to that teaching can keep prayer fresh.

A home group or Sunday School class can also be a great place for training more facilitators of corporate prayer. As the leader becomes more comfortable with this style of prayer, it would be great to have that leader begin asking others to be responsible for a season of prayer. The leader should meet with them and give them some ideas for a few times. During these meetings, the topic should move from just giving them the ideas of how a time of prayer could be structured, to helping them understand how to seek the Lord for their own ideas.

> **Blessed by Doing** – Without regard for what regularly happens in the weekend services, if you have responsibility for a group that meets regularly, apply what you have read above to your sphere of influence.

9.4 What about other special times of prayer?

Sunday School classes and home groups are great times for dynamic corporate prayer, but they don't have to be the only time. There are other times of prayer that can and should be taking place. Some of those times are elaborated below.

9.4.1 With vocational and volunteer staff

While I was pastoring a man challenged our leadership team to pray as much as we discussed issues. This turned into nearly 10 years of weekly prayer times for the elders of our congregation. Each week we ate a simple meal together, then prayed for about 45 minutes and talked for about 45 minutes. This entire section about how a congregation can grow in dynamic corporate prayer (Questions 9 – 9.3) should flow out of times when the leaders of a congregation pray together regularly. The life flow of both vocational and volunteer leaders will be greatly enhanced if the senior leader not only spends time with them in prayer regularly, but also seeks to equip them in more effective corporate prayer.

These times of prayer should be initiated and facilitated regularly by the senior leader. If that leader does not feel comfortable or equipped to lead this time, there are things they can do to become equipped and get more comfortable. The early church leaders gave themselves to "the prayer and the ministry of the Word." Just as giving oneself to the ministry of the Word must be a commitment for a senior leader of a congregation, so also should giving oneself to prayer. The ability of a senior leader to facilitate meaningful, dynamic corporate prayer should be expected by those who serve in the congregation. It is certainly appropriate for that leader to disciple and designate others to facilitate these times of prayer. But that should be as an enhancement to what normally happens, not a substitute for what should happen.

I want to reiterate at this point that I am not talking about the senior leader being the one who does all the praying, but rather that he facilitates the time of prayer so that all those involved will pray with greater purpose, direction, boldness, and confidence. There is no substitute for the senior leader modeling this process. And this is the best way to train others on the church staff.

A church in Birmingham, AL. has practiced dynamic corporate prayer for several years. Here is what their worship pastor writes.

We have found staff meetings to be a great time to train our entire staff team (including secretaries) on how to facilitate dynamic corporate prayer. We rotate responsibilities in that. Now every staff member is confident in that ability. We have had great success with our youth doing "sacred nights" once per month using dynamic corporate prayer. Our children are trained in Scripture-based prayer because our entire staff team sees it as valuable and is trained. We have created multiple Scripture-based prayer guides to help people in their personal and family times. Our Senior Pastor meets with our staff team every Sunday morning to pray through a passage from his sermon (either the main text or a corollary passage) just to listen in on what God may say through the team to incorporate into his message.

There are times when it is very appropriate that the prayers focus on the previous week. Based upon what was taught or what God did, it would be very right to look back, focus on a specific point or Scripture and pray. Other times it would be right to look forward in anticipation of what God may do, based upon the message that will be preached. Another option would be to pray for a specific segment of the congregation or a specific ministry. But no matter what the topic, again, the key to dynamic corporate prayer is that it is Spirit-led, worship-fed, and Scripture-based. Giving thought and prayer to these times of prayer, just as we would give to organization and administrative issues, will allow the leader to help people pray most effectively and also help them be equipped to facilitate other times of prayer.

➢ **Blessed by Doing** – Build times of dynamic corporate prayer into your staff meetings. Make it a priority to spend time together focusing on Jesus and praying from His Word. Pray for the needs of your congregation or ministry through Scripture passages that have recently or will soon be preached.

9.4.2 With leadership and ministry teams

What if each leadership team in your congregation, whether it is the elders, deacons, ushers, children's ministry, youth ministry or any other ministry, developed a similar practice as I mentioned above? What if they spent the same amount of time in prayer as they did discussing issues? These times of prayer could be for one another, the people they are serving, or for them to catch God's heart and direction for an aspect of the ministry.

I know of choirs who come together primarily to worship and pray, then the practice of the music fits into that context. The same is true with some worship teams I am familiar with. They spend much of their time praying – sometimes for each other, sometimes for the congregation, etc. – and worshipping. It is in that context that God gives them a sense of what they should be doing during their worship service.

What if the children's ministry team made it their priority to pray for each child under their care each time they gathered? Or if the youth team was lead by the youth pastor to pray for some specific needs based upon the message of the previous (or coming) week? In each of these cases, the prayer is not simply an introductory prayer, asking God's blessing on their meeting, but is seen as a key agenda item.

➢ **Blessed by Doing** – Make it a goal to equip those who have some ministry responsibility so they feel competent to facilitate this type of prayer.

9.4.3 Pre-service prayer

Whether it is for 5 minutes or 50 minutes, having a meaningful time of prayer prior to the Weekend Service is a statement by all involved in the service that they are not depending on their own efforts to accomplish the things God wants to do in and through them. The format of the prayer is not as important as the fact that it is happening.

This could be done in the different ministry teams (such as worship or greeters or youth or children's ministry teams) or it could be done all together. It is helpful if there is some specific prayer focus or Scripture given and an opportunity for many people to enter in. Again, the key thing is that the person facilitating this time of prayer takes time to ask the Lord how He wants the prayer time to go. You don't want to come to the time of prayer without some sense of how the group could pray and then find yourself a bit trapped into praying the way you prayed the last several times.

➢ **Blessed by Doing** – Consider how you can begin or enhance times of pre-service prayer. Consider a fresh approach regularly so it stays fresh.

9.4.4 Prayer during the service

It is a fairly well known story that Charles Spurgeon had many people praying for him each time he preached. He referred to this as his "furnace room." He attributed the success of his preaching to these pray-ers. One way to communicate the value of prayer in a congregation is to encourage prayer during the service. Even a casual reference to "those who are praying right now for this message" speaks volumes to the people in the congregation. There are several ways this can happen.

The most common approach that works especially well with multiple services is to ask people to gather together in a room to pray. If the pastor gives them some points to pray based upon the emphasis of his message, this can help them pray more specifically. If the pray-ers are able to watch a screen and/or hear the audio of what is happening in the service, they can add prayer for each part of the service, including the announcements, welcoming people, worship, as well as specific points of the worship and any type of call to respond to the message.

> *Even a casual reference to "those who are praying right now for this message" speaks volumes to the people in the congregation.*

I know of a congregation whose pastor assigns regular attenders to be pray-ers once or twice per year. They are *stealth* pray-ers who attend the service, but pray based upon a specific outline the pastor sends them beforehand. At times they pray for people around them, for people on the platform, for people who are not at the service, as well as for specific parts of the announcements and his message.

➢ **Blessed by Doing** – Ask the Lord if there are ways you should encourage prayer to take place during the service(s). If you have responsibility to help shape the weekend service, consider how this may look.

9.4.5 Seasonal – Such as Thanksgiving, Christmas, Easter, or Pentecost

Any special day can be a great *excuse* to encourage dynamic corporate prayer. It would be easy to find some Scripture verses or songs related to each of the days mentioned above. From there any of the prayer suggestions I have made for the times of corporate worship in Questions 9.2 and 9.3 above can apply. But the most important thing is for the person responsible for the service to take some time in preparation.

Take time to pray, asking the Lord how He wants it to look. Take time to ponder. Then *test pray* it. Take time to pray in the manner you anticipate asking others to pray. Then note what your experience was like. Did your suggestion help you pray better? Did it encourage a greater love for the Lord? If so, then perhaps it would do the same for the group you are leading. If not, perhaps it would be good to reconsider.

➤ **Blessed by Doing** – Look at the calendar and consider specific special days coming up. Which of those days would lend itself to some special prayer emphasis?

9.5 How can dynamic corporate prayer revive our weekly prayer meeting?

I appreciate the fact that many people are so committed to prayer that they hold onto and even fight for the weekly prayer meeting. But I don't think we should be so committed to the weekly prayer meeting that it becomes the *weakly* prayer meeting. Our commitment should be to make all the times of prayer fresh, meaningful, and dynamic. Prayer is so critical to God's overall plan that we dare not be satisfied with just going through the motions.

God prospers what we consider to be vital, what we seek Him for, what we prepare for, and what we have faith for. Guilt is always a poor motivator. This is especially true when it comes to prayer. Guilt that we should pray more may get people to a prayer meeting, but it will not keep them there. What will keep them excited about corporate prayer? When they encounter God.

We can't and we should not try to manufacture an encounter with God. In fact, I have found He doesn't cooperate very well when I try. But we can and should seek to establish an environment where He is welcome to come, lead, and manifest His glory. What does that environment look like? For specifics answers to this question, see Question 9.6 below. Look over those bullet points carefully.

Perhaps you could teach or discuss some of them before or at your prayer meetings. A regular time of prayer is a great opportunity to train people to come with expectation, to expect the Holy Spirit to give direction, to use Scripture as the basis of our prayer, and to let worship be that which fuels it.

> *What will keep them excited about corporate prayer? When they encounter God.*

It is important not to take away an important time and style of prayer that people appreciate. If you try to put new wine into an old wine skin, it is not just the new wine that is wasted, but the old wine skin is wasted as well. So, you may not want to bring vast changes to something that is already working well. But if there is agreement that new life is desired, then Spirit-led, worship-fed, Scripture-based, corporate prayer can bring that desired refreshing.

➢ **Blessed by Doing** – If your congregation has a regular, weekly prayer meeting, what have you read in this book that will help that time be vital and life-giving? Ask the Lord how to incorporate these things into your prayer times.

9.6 How can we establish a welcoming environment for God's presence?

He is under no obligation to follow any of our lists, but my experience has taught me that the following are key components for establishing an environment of vital connection with God.

- A desire to touch God's heart and honor His Son.
- Honest, open hearts of those who lead and those who pray.
- A commitment to pray in response to the Holy Spirit's leading rather than following a specific agenda.
- Times of thanksgiving and praise.
- A willingness to pray in fresh ways.
- Prayers that flow from Scripture.

- Prayers that focus more on God's ability instead of our need.
- Prayers to advance His kingdom rather than our desires.
- Worship and prayer mingled together.
- Pray-ers listening to one another and prayers that are connected.
- Anticipating God's creativity to show us fresh ways to connect with Him.
- Staying with a prayer topic until there is a sense that the group has prayed all they should on it.
- Shorter prayers rather than longer prayers.
- Pray-ers knowing they are in a safe place. That their honest prayers will not be shared with others.
- Great joy at a fresh awareness of some aspect of the character of God.
- Spirit-directed times of repentance and sorrow over sin.
- A facilitator who sees the value of corporate prayer and who is growing in his/her capacity to facilitate it.

When these elements define a time of corporate prayer, more people will sense the presence of God and will want to experience it more and more.

This type of prayer does not happen automatically. But it can happen regularly if the leader wisely applies what has been mentioned in this book and continues to seek God for how He wants the time of prayer to go and grow.

> **Blessed by Doing** – Which three of the bullet points above are happening best in your regular times of prayer? Which three would you like to have happen better? Ask the Lord to help you implement at least one of them.

10. Congregation, Part II – Should our congregation consider doing a Congregational Prayer Summit?

Acts 6:4 states that the two priorities of the early church leadership were prayer and the ministry of the Word. What would it be like if every congregation that valued the weekend proclamation of God's Word also valued meaningful, corporate prayer enough to have at least an annual prayer retreat? Would it help people become more mature in how they follow Jesus? Would it help your congregation become more of a "House of prayer?" Could it help bond more people together in a deep love for each other and for the Lord? I have seen each of these things happen.

10.1 What is a Congregational Prayer Summit?

One of the wonderful things God is doing in many congregations today is deepening the desire to become more devoted to prayer. Whether we call it becoming a "House of Prayer" or building a "culture of prayer" or being a "Prayer Saturated church", or being "devoted to prayer," or some other description, it is clear that God is calling more people to more prayer. In a time when the Wednesday Night Prayer Meeting is nearly a thing of the past, God has been stirring more and more of His people to build prayer into all aspects of their ministry.

> *What would it be like if every congregation that valued the weekend proclamation of God's Word also valued meaningful, corporate prayer enough to have at least an annual prayer retreat?*

The Moravian movement which began a one hundred year

prayer meeting and sent hundreds of people into the mission field beginning in the 1700's had a motto which said "No one ministers unless someone prays." This heart is being restored to the church today. The kind of prayer the Lord is restoring to His Church has two purposes: first to develop a deeper intimacy with the Lord and second to have a greater impact upon the world. One of the means God is using to build this kind of prayer into the life of congregations is through Congregational Prayer Summits.

Soon after Dr. Joe Aldrich began calling pastors in the Pacific Northwest to extended times of prayer he wrote out a definition of a Pastors Prayer Summit. The definition of a Congregational Prayer Summit which follows is an application of his definition to congregations.

A Congregational Prayer Summit is an extended, multi-day, life-changing worship experience attended by portions of a congregation whose sole purpose is to seek God, His kingdom, and His righteousness with the expectation that He will create and guide them through a humbling, healing, uniting process that will lead them to a unity of heart mind and mission and will qualify them for the blessing of God.

He also said that if he were pastoring again, Congregational Prayer Summits would be a must. Let's look at some of the phrases of this definition.

- First, it is an extended, multi-day time. Though it is wonderful to have a dynamic evening of prayer, a Prayer Summit simply requires more time away from the normal routines and responsibilities of life.
- It is also primarily a worship experience. There is much prayer that takes place, but the basis of the prayer is worship, not requests.
- It is attended by portions of the congregation such as men, women, leadership, couples, college age, etc.
- There are many valid reasons to come to God in prayer, but at a summit, the primary reason is simply to seek Him. Or, we could say it like Jesus did, "Seek first the kingdom of God and His

righteousness and all these things will be added unto you" (Matthew 6:33).

- We are not coming to Him to ask Him to bless our plans, but rather we are coming to Him to see if He will reveal any of His specific plans to us.
- But that does not mean we have no expectations of Him when we come. It is right that we would expect Him to meet us and guide us through a process which will include humbling us and uniting us and which will probably produce certain anticipated results.
- The primary result we anticipate is renewal in our relationship with Him as well as with those around us.
- In addition, we can anticipate Him leading us to a place where we can receive the blessing of more of His life poured out upon us.

We could also describe a Congregational Prayer Summit as an extended time of Spirit-led, worship-fed, Scripture-based, corporate prayer.

- It is "Spirit-led" as opposed to agenda or topically driven.
- It is "worship-fed" as opposed to request driven.
- It is "Scripture-based" as opposed to praying our own thoughts.
- It is "corporate prayer" as opposed to individual prayer in a group setting.
- It is prayer that is relational.
- It is prayer that comes out of corporate listening.
- It is prayer that reflects that we do not employ God, but rather He employs us.
- It is a time to seek the Lord in an unhurried, intentional manner, without a specific script.
- It is a time to be more interested in who God is than in what He can do; a time to seek His face more than to seek His hand.
- It is a time when we can spend prolonged, unhurried time with Him in the midst of His saints.

- It is a time to enjoy a flow of worship through singing, praying and the reading of Scripture.

We could see it as a time to simply be with Him (Mark 3:14, Acts 4:13). A time to take heed to our own heart (Proverbs 4:23, Acts 20:28). A time to be more like *Mary* and less like Martha (Luke 10:38-42).

The focus of a Prayer Summit is formation more than information. It is about establishing an environment more than doing an event. It is more about a process then the product. The prayer at a summit is more about delight than duty.

Let's also consider what a Congregational Prayer Summit is *not*. There are many worthy things a congregation does. Retreats and conferences have great value. But we would not encourage a congregation to have a Prayer Summit expecting it to be similar to another activity. A Prayer Summit will work best when it is not initiated because of curiosity but rather from conviction.

We also encourage you to fight the temptation to do a both/and event, trying to do both a Prayer Summit and a leadership retreat or a planning session, etc. at the same time. A Prayer Summit does not seem to work well as an add-on to another plan or agenda. Adding a session of summit-style prayer to a retreat is a very good thing, but that is different from a Prayer Summit. We encourage you to let it be a stand-alone time.

One the other hand, we encourage you to see a Prayer Summit as an integral part of a larger vision to help people enjoy a deeper relationship with Jesus Christ through prayer. A high quality Prayer Summit is not the goal. More of Jesus in the midst of your congregation is the goal. Prayer Summits have and can lead to increased relationship with Jesus and greater desire to pray. Although it is not the destination, it can be a very effective, unique wonderful vehicle to help get you to that goal.

10.2 Why should we consider a Congregational Prayer Summit?

There are five key words Dr. Joe Aldrich used to describe the process behind Pastors Prayer Summits. "The flow of God's grace begins with a fresh revelation of His *holiness*. Holiness produces *humility*. Humility is the precursor of *unity*. When unity is present, the city-wide church can be a *community* (*koinonia*). Where there is community, there is *impact*."

With these words in mind, a Congregational Prayer Summit provides an excellent environment for real congregational impact. It provides an excellent environment for a congregation to become a healthy community. It provides an excellent environment for congregational unity. It provides an excellent environment for individual and congregational humility. All of this is true because it provides individuals and the congregation an opportunity to spend extended quality time in the presence of a holy God.

In addition to these reasons, it is an excellent environment for people to learn corporate prayer through participation rather than explanation or observation. It provides an opportunity for both the leaders and the congregation to have a common knowledge and common experience related to prayer. It is a way congregational leadership can live out and demonstrate the biblical commitment to devote oneself to prayer (Acts 6:4). And it is the closest environment of what we know of NT church life (See 1 Corinthians 14:26).

What happens in our regular Sunday morning services is very good and necessary, but a Prayer Summit allows Jesus to be at the center and the pastor to facilitate the process of all the people looking at and moving toward Him. It allows all the people to participate and contribute to the flow of the meeting in a practical and meaningful way. It allows and encourages the various gifts and perspectives to be shared and appreciated. And it allows for flexibility without preset time con-

> *... but a Prayer Summit allows Jesus to be at the center and the pastor to facilitate the process of all the people looking at and moving toward Him.*

straints. So a season of prayer might last for 15 minutes or it may last for 2 hours.

➢ **Blessed by Doing** – Ask the Lord and others involved in the leadership of your congregation if it might be right to begin planning for a Congregational Prayer Summit. If so, consider the suggested steps below.

10.3 How would we plan a Congregational Prayer Summit?

"Once I see the value of a Congregational Prayer Summit, how do you go about making it happen in my setting?" There are several practical steps we would encourage you to follow.

The first and most significant step is that the pastor and the congregational leadership must have *a strong commitment and vision for greater intimacy and impact through prayer.* More than anything else, the dynamic of a congregational Prayer Summit will be affected by the vision. If the leadership of the congregation is not convinced a summit is an essential, divine vehicle to help them move forward in what God has called them to become, there is a danger it will not accomplish what it could accomplish. A Prayer Summit is not a magic pill that will cure all congregational ills.

Having said that, for a Congregational Prayer Summit to make a difference in your setting, the leadership needs to *recognize and appreciate the unique value of a Prayer Summit.* Although it is not a cure-all, it must be seen as a unique tool to accomplish God's purposes in your setting. God has seen fit to use the simple process of a group of hungry-hearted people getting away together with a deep desire to be with the Lord, enjoy Him, hear from Him and respond to Him. Though they do not have a route planned out to get where they want to go, they are convinced that the Guide will not only take them to their destination, but also that He Himself is their destination. They are convinced that even though they don't know what to do, their eyes should remain on Him (See 2 Chronicles

20:12).

Once the decision is made to have a Congregational Prayer Summit, *begin by praying for God's specific leadership and follow His directions!* He, more than anyone else, wants this time to be very meaningful to His people. The following are helpful suggestions, but seek Him and let Him be the one who gives leadership to this time. Following the Spirit of God is a key characteristic of a Prayer Summit. Therefore, it should also be a key part in getting there. It is helpful to talk to others about how they did it, but it is most helpful to talk to God about how He wants it done.

Determine the target group for the first Summit. There is value in several different options. You may feel led to start with the leadership, or with the men, or women. Because women are generally more responsive, you may want to give the men a bit of a running start! But be deliberate in your decision-making about this. Don't assume that God's direction for someone else is His direction for you. I would encourage the leadership of a congregation not to try to require all people from a group to attend. Though there are exceptions, generally speaking, those who receive the most from a Prayer Summit are there because they *want* to be there, not because they *have* to be there.

Share the vision (not the method) of greater intimacy with Jesus through Spirit-led, worship-fed, Scripture-based corporate prayer, etc. with the people. We would encourage you not to promote an event, but rather an opportunity to do that for which Jesus died; to develop a deeper love relationship with the Father through Jesus. If the Prayer Summit is promoted without the vision, it will be seen as only another nice, optional idea to take up a few more of my days and dollars. But if you lead with the vision of greater relationship with Jesus and present a Prayer Summit as an opportunity to help fulfill that vision, it will be seen as a vital part of the life of the congregation and the life of the individual as well.

Prepare and select facilitators. From a human perspective, this is the most important decision you will face. The quality of the facilitation will greatly affect the quality of the summit experience.

Please pray much about this. We encourage the pastor to participate as a facilitator. This is a wonderful opportunity to shepherd and disciple the people. If your summit is fairly large – say, about 60 or more people – you will probably want to have some times in smaller setting as well so that more people feel a freedom to participate.

Other facilitators could be either another pastor in your area who is experienced in dynamic corporate prayer or other congregational leaders the pastor has trained and developed. Facilitators should be people who have a heart to spend time with the Lord, know and value His Word, and also have enough people skills to know the basics of how groups function best. Simply because a person has a specific position in the church is not guarantee they will be a good Prayer Summit facilitator. See Sections 6-8 for more information on the facilitation process, and Question 10.4 on selecting facilitators.

Select a person to take care of the logistics. Perhaps he/she would chair a committee. Below are several things they will need to do or make sure get done.

Select dates – we strongly encourage you to have at least 2 ½ days away i.e. Thursday evening through Saturday evening, or Friday evening through Sunday afternoon. Please be very cautious about shortening the time to make it more convenient. And don't apologize for asking people to take some time off work. They have taken time off work for far lesser things than this. If it is worth doing, it is worth doing well. On the other hand, an overnight of prayer is better than no prayer at all.

Select a site – we strongly encourage you to find a place that is far enough away so that people do not come and go. Doing this at your own building can lose several dynamics. Make sure the site will suit your needs and desires in both space available and level of comfort. Make sure the contract is complete and signed. Dates, meals, minimum commitment, terms of cancellation, contact person, will all need to be addressed.

Communication/publicity – how will the word get out to the people? Testimonies are one of the strongest tools you have to use. For the first summit (before you have any of your own testimonies) you can use some from IRM's web site (www.prayersummits.net). Near the end of your first summit it would be good to give an opportunity for the participants to write out a testimony. Also, after the summit, give opportunity for testimonies to be given before the congregation. Begin building toward the second summit by the end of the first summit. If there is life at the first summit, others will know about it before the summits is over.

Set the cost – Think through the various additional expenses (scholarships for those in need and for those who serve, bus transportation, coffee and snacks, brochures/posters and other printing costs, any honoraria, etc.) and possible non-registration means of income (special offerings, gifts for scholarships, bake sales, etc.). The goal should be to have the Summit break even. It should not be used as a fundraiser for some other area of ministry, nor should it need to be funded by some other source.

Registration – Think through the registration process so that it works smoothly for all involved. You may want to have a team to pray for each participant before and during the summit. Consider providing something such as a prayed-over verse of Scripture or a small bag of chocolate, to make each person know that they are special in God's sight. Gathering email address is valuable. Even in smaller congregations there is value in using nametags. Think through how the money will be handled.

Communion – Often times God does some of His best work at summits around the communion table. You need someone to be responsible to make sure that the needed elements are there and set up at the right time. Sometimes there will be some needed preparation beyond the communion elements such as a table cloth, candles, flowers, etc. There are times when the use of a physical cross has added much to the atmosphere. You will want to think this through with the pastor so that it is taken care of when it needs to be.

Materials – To help everyone be able to enter into the summit experience as fully as possible, two specific resources can be very helpful, perhaps in a booklet form.

Song books or sheets (either purchased or put together). Arranging the songs in alphabetical order according to the first line allows people to find the song in the easiest manner. We strongly encourage you to follow copyright laws.

Several pages of material to assist times of personal and corporate prayer (such as the names, attributes of God, thoughts about pride and humility, a list of Scriptures on our identity, the "one another" commands, various topics for *concordance praying*, etc.) as well as a basic schedule, instructions and guidelines about the summit. See the resource page at www.uandibook.net for some examples.

The pastor should walk closely with this person(s) in the planning so that you are on the same page each step of the way. He should still feel the responsibility for all things related to the Prayer Summit, but having a group of people around him can free him to take care of other aspects of the summit such as sharing the vision and preparing facilitators, etc. But it is vitally important that the pastor stay in close connection with the person responsible for the logistics. You will want to talk about what activities may or may not be necessary or even appropriate.

Build a team of pray-ers who will pray before, during and after the summit. Since it is God who does

> *The pastor should walk closely with this person(s) in the planning so that you are on the same page each step of the way.*

the work at a Prayer Summit, it is very wise to coordinate a group of people who will be praying that the vision for what God wants to do at the summit will be accomplished. Prayer for the summit should not start when the summit starts. It should begin as soon as a team of pray-ers can be recruited. It would be good to have them pray about all the aspects of the summit – the dates, the location, the participants, the facilitators, etc. as well as have them praying during the summit itself.

Continually share the vision in many different settings (during individual conversations, in sermons, with the leadership, etc.). A Prayer Summit must be driven by the vision. Stating the vision once or in only one manner will not ignite the hearts to be involved. It would be good for the pastor to communicate the vision in many different ways – through letters, sermons, brochures, testimonies, personal phone calls and conversations, etc. If your heart is full regarding what God may do for His people through a summit, you will find yourself talking about it in many different settings.

Continue to pray and prepare your heart for greater intimacy with Jesus. The personal preparation of the pastor is also a vital part of the preparation. Continue to call out to God in your own personal times of prayer, not simply for other people who will attend the summit, but for your own heart as well. As you read Scripture, pray that the Lord will show you more of Himself and help you fall more deeply in love with Him.

10.4 Who should facilitate our Congregational Prayer Summit?

Facilitating people in dynamic corporate prayer is a key part of discipling them into all that Jesus commanded them to do. It is a great privilege to see people not only fulfill the specific commands of Scripture, but to see them grow as they encounter God.

Some of my most effective moments of ministry have been as I have been with others in this type of prayer. I remember wrapping up a Congregational Prayer Summit with a large group of men. The last morning, I invited people to share with a brief word or phrase what the last couple days had meant to them. Several people said things I expected. "Great worship." "Wonderful fellowship." "The beauty of unity." Etc. Then one man in the back said, "The best marriage seminar I have ever been to." I said to myself, "We didn't even talk about marriage! What is he referring to?" Then I realized that though we did not talk about marriage, Jesus had spoken to him about his marriage. And his life was changed.

I was in a congregation where this type of prayer had become a regular practice for many people. Over a couple days I heard several people mention that they were so thankful for their pastor because he had helped them fall more in love with Jesus through prayer. After I heard this comment a few times the thought came to me, "Every pastor in America should have the privilege of hearing this phrase over and over again."

So, I see that the best person to lead a Congregational Prayer Summit is the pastor of that congregation. It is appropriate that others may help. But if the senior leader of the congregation is not involved in facilitating this type of prayer they are missing one of the best opportunities of pastoring. This is an opportunity to lead by example, to let people see you and hear you pursuing God. As they see their pastor take these steps, they will be influenced to pursue Him too. Most pastors don't feel adequate to do this, because most pastors have not experienced it themselves. They don't have a point of reference.

> *"Every pastor in America should have the privilege of hearing this phrase over and over again."*

Two ways to overcome this are 1) simply going for it. Rely on the Lord, step out and do it. And 2) inviting someone else who is more experienced to help facilitate with you. More and more people are becoming experienced in facilitating dynamic corporate prayer. It would be very appropriate for the senior leader of a congregation to ask a friend who is experienced to help them. We at International Renewal Ministries would be happy to help you find someone who could assist in that process.

➢ **Blessed by Doing** – Feel free to contact us at if we can be of any encouragement or help in the process of training facilitators. www.prayersummits.net

11. Families – How can families make the best use of dynamic corporate prayer?

Even though most followers of Christ would argue that a "family altar" (by whatever name) is very desirable, few of us have been involved in a regular family time that has been meaningful or dynamic. When the desire for such a time moves us to the point of action, the model most available to us is a classroom setting. By default we try to recreate in our homes what we have seen in a church service. I am grateful there are some exceptions to this, but I am sad they are few. Even when we know we should do something and even when we want do it, it is still a difficult process to find what really works and fits into a family.

Dynamic corporate prayer can happen in families. It can happen with couples. It can begin with kids who are quite young. It can continue as kids grow through elementary age and through their teenage years. I know there is no "silver bullet" and no guarantees. But I also know that parents can make life-long, positive prayer memories with their kids.

Not long ago I had the privilege of being a "family prayer coach" to a family of six. This father and mother intentionally decided they wanted each of their four kids (ages 5 to 11) to grow in their prayer lives, individually and collectively. Dad and Mom were not asking me to fix their kids. They already were a good, strong family. But they all wanted to grow more in prayer. We agreed to meet for four sessions over a period of about 6 weeks.

The Lord's Prayer was the bases of our time together. They came away saying that prayer was turned from a mystery to a fun family experience. Now their best times of prayer are when they have a time of giving thanks, or when they use the Lord's Prayer as a pattern. Part of what I shared with them was how this prayer could provide some structure for their prayers. We contrasted the requests of the two halves of the prayer. We practiced praying "on earth as it is in heaven" after each of the first three requests. I also showed them a chart of how Martin Luther used this prayer as a tutorial for his daily prayer.[28]

The father of this family told me recently that they don't always pray through the pattern of the Lord's Prayer, but when they do, it is always a good time for their family. They said they were blessed, but I was the one who came away with a deeper appreciation for each of them as well as a deeper excitement to keep investing in as many young families as possible. If the desire is there, there are many ways the Lord can use to make progress.

➤ **Blessed by Doing** – Honestly evaluate your commitment to influence your family's ability to pray effectively together. If it is not as high as you want it to be, the place to start is to ask God for His heart and help.

11.1 What is the role of parents and grandparents in dynamic corporate prayer?

Sometimes it is not possible, but whenever it is, it is God's desire for moms and dads to teach their children about all aspects of a healthy relationship with the Lord, including the role of prayer. Simply put, God is trusting parents to accurately reflect and teach their kids about who He really is. This is one of their foremost responsibilities.

The first key component is the desire and commitment to accept this responsibility. Without this there will be no lasting fruit. If the desire is not there, the best place to start is to recognize that and ask the Lord for the desire to do His will in this area.

If one parent has the desire to teach their children and the other does not, then you have a starting point. Even though it is best to

---

[28] See footnote 1 on page 38.

have both dad and mom involved in the process, it is not a requirement. Whoever has the desire should take whatever steps they can.

The desire I am referring to is not for a successful program or for even a few successful times of spiritual instruction. It is a long-term desire to have your kids become fully responsible adults who have a dynamic, growing relationship with Jesus. Programs will come and go. Ideas that work well at one stage will not work well at another stage. But what is necessary at each stage is the deep desire that your kids would love the Lord with all their heart, soul, mind, and strength.

Grandparents can also play a very significant role in this process of raising godly children. Some grandparents may initiate the topic, and some may need to be asked. Either way grandparents can have a great impact upon the spiritual development of their grandchildren. If the natural grandparents have no desire to be involved in this or if, for whatever reason, they are not in the child's life, then you have a great opportunity to adopt some grandparents for your children. Unlike the first time, this time you get to choose!

> *What is necessary at each stage is the deep desire that your kids would love the Lord with all their heart, soul, mind, and strength.*

> ➢ **Blessed by Doing** – Are you fulfilling your God-given role in the lives of your kids or grandkids by teaching them to pray most effectively? Write out a few things you are doing well and a few areas where you need help.

11.2 How can we help young children get started in dynamic corporate prayer?

How do we help young children get started in understanding and feeling comfortable praying with others? The two best times in the day to do this are meal time and bed time. These are two natural times when parents and kids interact. Making use of these two times will get you well down the road.

Whether is it with just one child or many children, when you sit down at a table for a meal, instead of praying the same way all the time, why not change it up a bit? Doing the same thing over and over may establish a nice tradition, but the meaning can diminish. Even changing things physically helps. For example, instead of praying while you are sitting down, have everyone stand behind their chair during prayer. Or instead of holding hands to pray, why not ask everyone to lift their hands in prayer? Instead of just thanking God, "for the hands that prepare this meal" why not actually gather around the cook and express thanks to the Lord for her/him.

> *The two best times in the day to do this are meal time and bed time.*

At our table when our grandkids are with us, I rarely ask, "Who wants to lead us in prayer?" Instead I say, "Who gets to pray tonight?" Often times it is more than one grandkid who wants to pray. We have tried to make it fun. There are times when I will say, "Tonight, we are all going to pray" and I will ask them to repeat the words after me. Or, I will ask someone else to lead us and we follow them, phrase by phrase. Other times, I will have us keep our eyes open and look at one thing they are thankful for then complete the sentence, "Tonight I am thankful for ____." Or you could pray at the end of the meal rather than at the beginning.

Similar methods can be used at bedtimes. As you pray, lead the child in prayer, rather than just praying for them. Select a topic, or read a verse or mention a person, and talk for just a minute about how to pray so their prayers can be a positive experience. You could do some "ping-pong" prayer where you take turns back and forth mentioning one thing you like about God, or thank Him for.

But it is not just meal time and bed time that can be used. Marilyn and I volunteered to help in the AWANA program at a nearby church so our grandkids would be involved. During the opening time, I noticed that when kids were asked to pray they were eager to respond, but then seemed to stumble or wander when it came time to pray. So, we began to "coach" the kids in prayer. When it was their turn to pray, we would stand right next to them, say a phrase for them, and they would repeat it after us. We were acting as training wheels for them. This helped them pray with more confidence and it also helped them pray prayers more related to the purpose of the time instead of about anything that popped into their minds at the time.

Spontaneous times of prayer can be very teachable moments. Many years ago we had a foster son live with us for 10 months. He had his 7th birthday with us. The first Sunday he was with us we had communion at our church. When the elements came by, I passed them around him to my wife. He was curious and asked why he couldn't have some. Later that afternoon as I explained the significance of Jesus' death to him, he prayed after me and asked Jesus to be His Savior.

When our grandkids spend the night with us, besides praying with them at night, they will sometimes wake up while I am praying in the morning. On many occasions I have included them in my prayers. I will call them over to sit on my lap and generally keep praying on the topic I have been on, but include them in the process.

At this point Marilyn and I have seven grandkids. Six of them are young and live near to us. Each year we take them to "Cousins' Camp." To come to cousin's camp, you have to be one of our grandkids, be at least three years old, and be potty trained! This Friday-Monday is a time Marilyn and I put a lot of effort into. We want them to think this is the best weekend of their whole year. We take them to a piece of property we have owned for many years that has a 35 foot travel trailer on it. It is our get-a-way spot. It is sort of half camping and half RV-ing.

Our main goal during these days is to invest in their spiritual lives. So, throughout the day we do stories and activities with a purpose. Prayer is a key part of Cousin's Camp. We have encouraged them to pray not only at meal times, but at other points throughout the day. Some are planned, some are spontaneous. There are times when we have asked them to pray for each other. When someone gets hurt we have gathered around and prayed for that person. At night we typically lay on a blanket near the campfire, look up at the stars and talk about how big and great God is. We try to mix prayer into the fabric of all the things we do.

We are also "bribing" our grandkids to memorize Scripture by giving them a shiny new gold dollar for every verse they memorize.

> *We try to mix prayer into the fabric of all the things we do.*

When they have a verse to say to me, I try to make it a big deal. We go to the most formal part of our house. I ask them for the reference of the verse. They quote the verse for me. Then we talk about it and find some way to pray from that verse. Our hope is that they will grow up knowing that the Bible is the best book ever and the best prayer book ever.

> **Blessed by Doing** – What ways have you helped younger children pray more confidently? Try one of the things you have read above with your kids or grandkids. Or (better yet) ask the Lord how you can do it in your setting and take another step. Make good use of meal times and bed times. If you don't have kids or grandkids close by, consider *adopting* some.

11.3 How can we keep teenagers engaged in dynamic corporate prayer?

If you start when the kids are young, it is a natural thing to continue to pray together when they are teenagers. You just need to stay out of ruts by thinking about the best way to pray for their current age. If, for whatever reason, you did not pray with your kids when they were in preschool or elementary school, it is not too late to start!

Obviously the most important prayer is one of surrendering to the Lordship of Jesus. If your kids have not prayed to ask Jesus to be their Lord and Savior, that is the place to start. If they do have a desire to follow Christ, and you have not been praying with them, here is what I suggest. Set up a special time to get together. Perhaps go get a burger or go for a drive. Confess to them that God has convicted you of something you should have been doing since they were young. Don't make it dramatic, but make it real. Then tell them you would like to pray together far more regularly than you have in the past. Tell them you are looking forward to learning together.

As you engage in prayer, do not pray long prayers! Don't preach at them in your prayers. Don't try to impress them by using fancy language or complex ideas when you pray. Pray about things that really matter to you and your kids. Pray simple, perhaps even one topic, prayers. Use everyday language. But most of all, be authentic. Read a verse of Scripture and pray around one or two ideas from that verse. Or you may want to say, "I have been thinking about your friend. It seems like their family may be going through a hard time right now. Can we pray for them? How do you think would be the best way to pray for them?"

> *Then tell them you would like to pray together far more regularly than you have in the past.*

You will also want to have times of prayer when you focus only on who God is and what He wants to do. Have times when you express thanks to Him. Have times when you read some Scripture about His greatness and pray from those verses.

And if you have been praying with them since they were young, or when you are feeling comfortable praying together, it is still a good plan to make good use of meal time and bed time. Only now you will probably be going to bed before them!

With just a little bit of thought, you can pray in fresh, creative ways and at fresh, creative times. Ask the Lord to give you ideas. Ask your friends what has worked best for them. Adapt ideas.

Make them yours. Pray prayers of thanksgiving, prayers of intercession, prayers of worship, prayers for help. Take the ideas of Spirit-led, worship-fed, Scripture-based prayers mentioned in this book and adapt them to fit your unique family situation.

My friend, Kevin Moore, has given us a great resource. Kevin and his congregation have been very intentional at helping families engage in dynamic corporate prayer. He has developed a website which gives specific ways for families to pray from Scripture. http://www.yourhomeahouseofprayer.com/ has many resources worth checking out.

➤ **Blessed by Doing** – Make sure that each of your kids is seriously considering asking Jesus to be Lord and Savior of their lives. Don't assume this. Talk and pray with them and for them so their relationship with Jesus is well established in their lives.

➤ **Blessed by Doing** – What has been the best way you have you prayed with teenagers (yours or someone else's)? Take one suggestion mentioned above and try it as you pray with them.

Various Questions

12.1 What are some hindrances to dynamic corporate prayer?

The primary hindrances to dynamic corporate prayer have nothing to do with a person's love for the Lord, or their maturity level, or their giftedness.

The primary hindrance is a lack of familiarity with this model of praying. We need *a renewed experience of prayer.* This type of prayer relies much more on listening than it does on lists. It allows us to approach our Father through prayer with a freshness and a confidence. This is *get to* prayer, not *have to* prayer.

We rarely move beyond our past experience without exposure to something new. Most pastors (and other prayer leaders) have not been taught to lead prayer like this. They have not seen it modeled. They have not participated in it. It is not so much that they have rejected it as it is that they have not had an opportunity to embrace it. Therefore, most parishioners have only been exposed to what I would call, "individual prayer in a group setting."

We also need *a renewed concept of prayer.* I once heard Dr. Alvin VanderGrind describe the *progression* of prayer. That is, how our concept of prayer changes as we mature. Below is what he shared, with my additions at points along the way.

> *We rarely move beyond our past experience without exposure to something new.*

We should move from seeing prayer as…

- Asking God for things or to do things.
- To: Talking to God.

- To: Communicating with God.
- To: The communication part of a relationship with God.
- To: The most important part of my relationship with God.
- To: The most important part of my love relationship with God.
- To: The most important part of the most important love relationship I have.
- To: The most important part of the most important love relationship I have with the Most Important Person in the universe!
- And finally to: *Enjoying* the most important part of the most important love relationship I have with the Most Important Person in the universe!

I am very aware that one key aspect of prayer is to see His purposes accomplished on earth as it is in heaven. Another aspect of prayer is to move into a deeper, more submitted and loving relationship with our Heavenly Father. To the degree that we view prayer as a relational experience, to that same degree we will develop more capacity and hunger for dynamic corporate prayer. See more on the importance of how we view prayer in Question 2.3.

A third hindrance is that we often feel like we *need to control the prayers* in a public setting. It can get too risky if we don't! I understand this appropriate desire, but I am also convinced that this perspective has led us to need a renewed trust in the Lord and His Church. There certainly are times when it is inappropriate to let anyone pray anything they may want to pray. And, given some brief instructions, there are other times when it is inappropriate that we not let anyone pray.

In addition to these three primary hindrances, my experience has taught me there at least three other reasons why more prayer leaders don't move in dynamic corporate prayer.

- *A lack of security/confidence in themselves* – we are not sure what might happen so our option is to not let anything happen.
- *A lack of creativity* – we have found a method that seems to work well so we have no sense of need to do anything diff-

erently. We don't want to be creative simply to do something differently, but we don't want our lack of creativity to hinder us from knowing more fresh ways the Lord might have for us and our group to pray. See more on the place of creativity in Question 7.3.

- *A lack of instruction* – much of the time, when this one is addressed – when someone is taught a different way to pray –it seems to remove the other hindrances as well. In fact, my hope is that this book will help address this hindrance.

  ➢ **Blessed by Doing** – What other hindrances have you come across as you have facilitated corporate prayer? I would love it if you sent me a note through the web site with your question so we could address it in the future.
  www.uandibook.net

12.2 What is the *most dangerous* and what is the best facilitation activity you know of?

All prayer activities are not of equal value. Some hit the mark, some don't.

Do you remember the illustration I gave in Question 4.2 about asking a group to write a Psalm? Let me tell you what happened after that great time of worship.

As we moved from there to lunch, I was reflecting on what had just happened. In my mind's eye, I was folding that suggestion up and ready to put it in my back pocket. The words never really formed in my mind, but the idea was, "I am going to keep this one! That way, if the Lord does not come through for me sometime in the future, I will just pull this one out again and it will work just as well!"

About the time I was beginning to think this, the Lord spoke to me in a very clear way. It was one of those times when what He said almost had quotation marks around it. "You can do that, but it would be one of the most dangerous things you could do."

You see, the reason this prayer activity worked so well was not because I was such a great facilitator and had such a great idea at just the right time! The reason it was effective was because I was listening at the right time, and He was gracious enough to share with us one little aspect of what was going on in Heaven and how we could enter into it at that time.

> *"You can do that, but it would be one of the most dangerous things you could do."*

Therefore, one of the most dangerous ways we can facilitate the next time of prayer is by doing something that worked really well the last time. Again, the reason this is *dangerous* is because we may be leaning on our own understanding and not pressing into and listening to Him.

This is not to say that we should never use a prayer activity more than once. But it does mean that we should not come with some kind of plan that is a substitute for seeking God for what He wants done in that place at that time.

On the other hand, the *best* prayer activity is the one you are confident He is leading you into. The idea may be one you have used on many occasions or it may be the very first time you have ever heard of it. If you have a question about the appropriateness or the timing of the activity, you may want to ask a trusted co-facilitator or friend in the group. The Lord may not communicate it or confirm it in the same way He has done it in the past. But when it becomes evident that He is leading and the group is following, you will see wonderful *God-moments* happen.

➢ **Blessed by Doing** – Have you tried to reproduce a fresh work of the Lord? If so, have you repented of it yet? Commit to the Lord that you will seek to always stay fresh with Him and not try to reproduce His last very effective act. This does not mean you can never make use of the same prayer activity more than once. But it does mean you will only do so if you sense the Holy Spirit is directing you.

12.3 How can sharing in Communion enhance times of dynamic corporate prayer?

The most meaningful experiences I have had in corporate prayer have come around a communion table. The cross of Jesus is the apex of history. If Jesus had not gone to the cross, there would be no need for the Bible! What would God have to say to us? The cross is the place where righteousness and peace kiss (Psalm 85:10). It is the act that tore down the dividing wall (Ephesians 2:14). It is the greatest expression of God's great love for us (Romans 5:8). Jesus will be known throughout eternity as the "Lamb that was slain." He is the "Once-for-all Sacrifice." Everything we need to know about who God is can be seen by looking at the cross.

When we enter into worship around the cross, we are on high and holy ground. The cross is the primary reason why Jesus is exalted and why Heaven rejoices. As we, His redeemed people, gather together to join with all creation and stand in wondrous awe at this greatest-of-all act of love, we can enjoy an encounter with the Living God that rarely comes through any other means. My experience has shown that Jesus seals His work, gets our attention, drills down deeper, brings both brokenness and healing, and grants freedom to our lives as we focus on the cross. Because the cross is so precious to the Father, Son, and Holy Spirit, some of the most precious times in prayer I have witnessed have come as we linger there.

I had the privilege of sharing communion with some Bible School students in Moscow, Russia. We had spent two weeks going through Paul's letters and the last afternoon we took time to receive the Lord's Supper. I shared a bit that we often (and rightly) remember Jesus in His earthly life when we come to this table. But this time I encouraged them to remember how Jesus had touched them personally. I invited them to come to the table, pick up a piece of bread and a cup, and speak directly to Jesus beginning their prayer with the words, "Jesus I remember when…" and then fill in some specific details.

During this time, I only cried once. It began soon after the first person began sharing and it concluded about 45 minutes later when the last person completed their prayer. These young, committed ministers shared comments like, "Jesus, I remember when You came to us when my father was taken from our family because he was a Christian. I remember how You sustained him while he was beaten and how You sustained us while he was away." Or, "Jesus, I remember when You were so present with me when I was being beaten. You allowed me to have the grace not to hate those who were beating me." It continued on and on. I was listening through a translator, but I could tell that all of us in the room were deeply moved.

> *During this time, I only cried once. It began soon after the first person began sharing and it concluded about 45 minutes later when the last person completed their*

In other settings I have encouraged groups to do a similar process. Though it has not been as deep as the time in Moscow, it has always been a very meaningful time.

As a friend of mine was facilitating a Prayer Summit he was told about "the feud" that "everyone in town knew about." It was something that happened between two significant churches from two different denominations. And it had lasted for over ten years! That night, after some interaction with key people from those churches and denominations, they conducted a funeral service for the feud. Two key people, representing the two sides of the conflict, stood hand-to-hand over the communion table and prayed. They buried the feud and prayed blessing upon each other.

Here are some things to consider as you weave prayer into a time of remembering the cross.

- You may want to consider an entire session of prayer focusing on the cross. So often it seems to be added on to another service. It really does warrant our exclusive attention. Take time to linger in His presence.

- There are so many ways to set up and participate in communion. Take time to ask the Lord, take time to ponder, what would be the most effective way to do it *this* time. The way it happened last time may not be the best way this time. The group can receive it together. Individuals can come to the table one by one or they could bring someone else, or even come as a small group of people. You may want people to serve one another. It can be very meaningful to suggest that people serve many other people. Have a large amount of bread and cups on the table and encourage them to share the elements and pray with several others. This allows people to express their love and the Lord's love for one another in a unique manner.

- Consider how you can help people *participate* – that is a great translation of the Greek word *koinonia* from which we get the word *communion* – during this time. Help them be active players rather than passive observers. Perhaps have several people express thanks – this is another great translation of the word *Eucharist* – for the broken body and the shed blood of Jesus. Remember to keep it fresh.

- There are many songs that focus on the cross or on His love expressed at the cross. Encouraging the group to sing several of these songs establishes a great atmosphere for receiving the bread and the cup. As this happens, the Holy Spirit may put an emphasis on a specific song or truth. Be sensitive to Him in the process. And move with those promptings to linger in prayer around a specific truth.

- There are many Scripture references about the cross or the blood of Jesus. I call these *cross references*. It is easy to develop a list within just a few minutes from a concordance by looking up "cross" or "blood." You can do many things with this list. Make use of what I wrote about *concordance praying* in Question 5.3 as you consider this list. Stirring Scripture with prayer at the table is a powerful combination.

- Whatever your theological position is on the meaning of this act, consider using only Biblical words to describe the bread and the cup. This may be a bit of a challenge because of the familiarity of our phraseology, but it is well worth it to keep things fresh. This is especially helpful in a multi-denominational setting.

• Ask the Lord how He may want to conclude the time at the table. Are there prayers of blessing one another to be prayed? Are there prayers of thanksgiving to be prayed? It has been very meaning when I have asked people to stand and gather around the table and pray a very short prayer of gratitude for the cross. Or, to speak in a word or short phrase what Jesus was sharing with them as we shared in communion.

Remembering Jesus and His work on the cross in a corporate setting has a great power to draw people into a deeper unity and to draw out more passion for Jesus.

➢ **Blessed by Doing** –The next time you are responsible to lead communion, view it as an opportunity for much participation by the people. Ask God if there is a new way to introduce or to participate in this wonderful reminder of Jesus' greatest act.

12.4 How do times of silence and non-verbal prayer fit into dynamic corporate prayer?

We live in a noisy world. When there are people together, if there is not talking going on we think we must be in a library. When we are listening to the radio or watching television whenever we exper- ience, "dead air" we know something is not right. Because of this, sometimes when we pray, silence can get a bit awkward. One of the elements of dynamic corporate prayer is that silence really can be golden.

When we give each other permission to enjoy a time of silence, or when we give a brief explanation about what God may want to do during a time of silence, these times can be deeply moving. So, letting people know ahead of time that a period of silence is okay and letting them know that this may be a time when God is doing a deep work will help turn it from a possible time of awkwardness to a time of anticipation.

Oftentimes, silence happens after a time of deep and wonderful worship or adoration of the Lord. After we sing, read, and pray, it seems the only thing left is to just stand in His presence and enjoy it. Or it may come when the group comes to a clear conclusion on a topic of prayer. During these times, we don't need to try to fill the vacuum just because it is there. I have heard stories of several wonderful things like this take place during a time of silence.

- People enjoy a deep, abiding sense of His presence.
- God speaks deeply into their heart about His great love for them.
- People become unaware of other people and their surroundings and it seemed it was just the Lord and them.

> *After we sing, read, and pray, it seems the only thing left is to just stand in His presence and enjoy it.*

- People become very aware of other people, but it didn't matter.
- God brings healing or a deep sense of resolution to a situation.
- God answers a question that has been on the person's heart.

Whenever it comes, whether it is intentional or more spontaneous, if people are not afraid of it, God can accomplish much through silence. As one who is responsible for the time of prayer, you will want to consider how and when a time of silence should be recognized.

➤ **Blessed by Doing** – Using some of the bullet points above, instruct the people in your prayer group about the value of times of silence. Help them remain engaged even when it is silent.

12.5 Should we use various settings – individual, small group, large group – during our prayer time? If so, how?

It is very helpful to use a variety of settings for corporate prayer. Familiarity is good, but the distance between over-familiarity and a rut is too often too close. Three settings form a great balance to a time of corporate prayer. Much of the time will be spent in a large group setting. You want everyone to be able to hear and see each other so, setting chairs in either one circle or in concentric circles (depending upon the size of the group) works well for this time. Singing works best in this setting.

But not everyone will pray in this larger setting, so smaller groups of anywhere between 5 and 25 can also be used as well. There should be a specific reason for shifting from the large group to the smaller group. Perhaps it is just to allow more people to enter in, or to pray for one another – this works best in groups smaller than 8-10 – or to pray through a passage or a series of verses. You may want to assign a more mature person from each group to make sure the reason for the group is accomplished. And it will also be important to think through any suggested instructions before you move into smaller groups.

One of the great joys of corporate prayer times is praying for one another. If this is the purpose of the small group time, there are a variety of ways this could happen. Typically, we ask a person how they would like us to pray for them. But perhaps a better way is to have the person who will be prayed for simply pray his/her requests to the Lord. There are several benefits to this.

First of all, we communicate in a different and better way when we are talking directly to the Lord rather than talking to one another.

But perhaps a better way is to have the person who will be prayed for simply pray his/her requests to the Lord.

It also allows the people who will be praying to hear the heart of the one they will be praying for instead of just the words. Furthermore, when we share our requests before we pray, the time of sharing can eat up the time of praying. So it is often a better use of the time. This process also encourages the other pray-ers to consider more carefully what is being prayed rather then what they are going to pray about.

As we pray in this way, it is essential that people know they are in a safe environment. We must give each other the gift of confidentiality. And we want to make sure that we pray "for" them not "at" them. We may want to remind the pray-ers that this is not a time to counsel or instruct the person being prayed for, but to pray God's grace upon them. We all need people to stand with us at key points in our life and bearing one another's burdens through prayer is a very meaningful way to do so.

Often times, especially in more extended times of prayer, a way to encourage deep and open sharing of real needs is to ask people to picture their lives in concentric circles with their relationship with Jesus as the bull's eye of the target, their spouse in the next circle out, other family beyond that, and their work and/or ministry beyond that. The desire for this time of prayer is that we get as close to the center as possible. This is not a time to pray about other people's needs, but rather to share what is really going on in one's own life and humbly ask for prayer.

I remember a time at a Prayer Summit many years ago when a pastor sat in a chair in the middle of the room and poured out his heart about a very difficult family situation. Several other pastors gathered around him ready to pray for him. Just before we began to pray Dr. Joe, who was facilitating the time, said, "Just a minute here." Then he pointed to the person in the chair and asked, "What denomination are you with?" The man answered through his tears. Then he went around the circle and asked each person ready to pray the same question. None of the people ready to pray for this pastor was part of his denomination. Then he pointed back to the man in the chair and asked, "Do you care what denomination they are?" When real needs are presented and prayed for in this manner, unity is the natural result.

Ask the Lord how you can encourage meaningful prayer for one another. *The chair* has been seen as a model of the mercy seat, where Jesus comes as the mediator and extends His mercy to us who need mercy. Or, as the Father's lap, where His "kids" can climb up into it and enjoy a deeper level of fellowship with Jesus as we whisper things to Him and He whispers back. As you invite this level of prayer you may want to make sure you have a supply of "ministry towellettes" – otherwise known as tissues – available. Tears often are the part of God's cleansing or watering process. There is more on *the chair* in Question 12.6 below.

Individual times can be a very important encounter during the wider corporate prayer experience. But, again, there should be some reason for these times. Here are some factors that can make individual times very refreshing.

- Select a section of Scripture, a series of verses, or a topic and encourage people to pray through it.
- If you do this, you may want to let them know that when they return you will invite them to continue to do in the large group setting what they have been doing individually.
- Perhaps they just need time to get alone with God and pray about things they don't normally pray about or things they sense they should pray about more.
- Depending on the setting, encouraging people to take a walk with Jesus will allow them to pray on topics they otherwise might not.
- You may sense you should send people out two by two to spend time simply exalting Jesus to each other. Encourage them to speak to one another only about some aspect of Jesus. I see this as "boasting in the Lord." Because this is different than what we normally do, it can require some very specific instructions and some extra discipline to stay on topic.
- Making use of the discipline of silence can also enhance these individual times. This may also take some specific instruction because we are not used to being silent as we are coming and going.
- If the physical setting (and the weather) allows for it, you may want to make use of being outside for a session of prayer. I have wonderful memories of walking on a beach, around a lake,

up to a high hill, or through a wooded trail during times of individual prayer.

- During this time, you may want to encourage short *breath* prayers of agreement with Scripture. For example...
  o Let Your name be holy through my life
  o Let Your kingdom come in all the areas of my life
  o Let Your will, not my will be done
  o I will bless You, Lord, at all times
  o Release Your grace in and through my life
  o You are my Shepherd
  o The earth is Yours and all it contains
- Or you may want to encourage them to do a similar thing around giving thanks.

➤ **Blessed by Doing** – Don't always use the same setting when you pray. Use smaller groups to their full advantage. Be sensitive to the Lord so the setting helps accomplish His purposes.

12.6 What about the chair and praying for each other?

One of the greatest gifts we can give to each other is the gift of our need by asking them to pray with us. One of the greatest gifts we can receive is the gift of our heart-felt prayers. And one of the most effective ways I have engaged in prayer for others is what has become known in Prayer Summit circles as *the chair*. The typical room arrangement of a Prayer Summit is in concentric circles. At a time when it is right to be praying for each other, often a chair is placed in the middle of the room and people are invited to come and share the gift of their need and receive prayer.

This time can be viewed and introduced in a variety of ways. For example, the chair can be referred to as the "Father's Lap" that He is inviting His child to climb upon, share what is happening, and listen to the Father's perspective. Or, it has been referred to as the "Mercy Seat." This is a place where the needy can come and receive mercy. Or it has been seen as a "Safety Zone" where a person can pray whatever they want to and know that they are really safe.

This seems to work best with brief instructions like the following.

- You are invited to come, pray, and be prayed for.
- This is a time to "bear one another's burden" as expressed in Galatians 6:2. It is not a time to pray *at* someone, instruct them, or to correct them, but to pray *with* and *for* them.
- When you'd like, please come to the chair and simply begin praying. Others are invited to gather around you at any time.

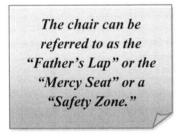

The chair can be referred to as the "Father's Lap" or the "Mercy Seat" or a "Safety Zone."

- They will listen to your prayer and therefore know what your requests are.
- When you are through praying, they will join you in your prayer. They will pray prayers of agreement with you, or read and pray from some appropriate Scriptures.
- Let's make sure that everything you hear here is held in complete confidence. It needs to be a safe place.

Then, you may want to enter into a time of worship or more prayer and just let the chair be available to anyone whenever they want to come. There can be some variation on this and let the time be directed by the Holy Spirit. Based upon how I have watched Him meet people in this setting, I think it must be one of the His favorite times of prayer.

When someone prays a prayer that others can relate to, you may want to invite others to come and be prayed for at the same time. For example, if someone is praying about a child, or grandchild who is not following the Lord, or if someone is praying for a spouse who is struggling in some manner, you may want to say, "If others of you relate to this request and want to be prayed for, we invite you to come and join them here."

An observation I remember hearing from a trusted, experienced woman facilitator is that when men go to the chair, generally the issue is sin – their sin or the effects of the sin of another. But when women go to the chair, generally the issue is hurt. For this reason, and because we want to establish an environment where the deepest ministry can take place, it is best to have these times of ministry be gender specific with the men praying together and the women praying together. A possible exception to this may be when couples are praying for couples. But even in this setting you may want to have it be gender specific.

➢ **Blessed by Doing** – Consider having a season of prayer following *the chair* model mentioned above. Introduce it by saying you are going to try something new this week.

12.7 Is there a place for teaching and instruction during times of dynamic corporate prayer?

Jesus took advantage of various settings to teach significant things. He taught about Living Water to a woman who was thirsty. He taught about catching people instead of fish to fishermen. It was to people whose minds were on food that He taught about the Bread that comes down out of heaven. Though there is a place for systematic, lengthy instruction, spontaneous, brief instruction is a very powerful teaching tool.

In a similar way, a skilled facilitator will recognize teaching opportunities. These should not be lengthy preaching times that will take away from the prayer. But rather they should be succinct times that intentionally lead people into more and better prayer.

An older pastor was at a Prayer Summit. People were reading Scriptures and praying on the topic of humility. In this setting of prayer, this wise man began sharing from four Scriptures about Paul's "descent into greatness." He first mentioned that in Galatians 1 and 2, one of Paul's earliest letters, he argues his claim to apostleship. Then in 1 Corinthians 15:9 he refers to himself as the "least of the apostles." Later, in Ephesians 3:8 he sees himself as "less than the least of all God's people." And finally in1 Timothy 1, at the end of his life, he describes himself as the worst sinner who ever lived. Then he prayed. What he prayed related to what he shared. And what he shared came out of a life well lived.

In a few short moments much teaching had taken place. Pastors around the room were scrambling for pen and paper to take notes. It was a lesson that people will remember for years. In fact, I am sure those in the room found a way to weave it into at least one of their sermons.

In another setting, the Lord led us to read John 13 toward the end of two days together in prayer. As someone read that, I was struck with the phrase in the first verse, that Jesus, "now showed them the full extent of His love." After the brother read the section of Scripture, I came back and shared briefly what the Lord was pointing out to me from this line. I described how the disciples must have sat up straighter and listened more carefully because whatever was coming next was going to be a huge act of love! When they saw Jesus get up and wash their feet, some of them could have wondered, "that's it? The full extent of His love is that He washes our feet?" I said that they probably didn't under-stand the place and power of servanthood any more than we do.

Pastors around the room were scrambling for pen and paper to take notes.

We then spent time praying around the theme of servanthood. Just before we all left the summit, a key leader in the city reflected back to that moment and said, "What I am taking home is, 'the full extent of His love.'" Everyone recognized the key truth Jesus had taught us.

In just a few minutes very significant truth had been transferred. Neither this elderly pastor nor I "prepared a message." We just shared what God was pointing out to us from our own observation or from what He had already put into our lives. When shared in a manner that flows with what God is doing, these can prove to be very meaningful times of instruction.

Also, a simple, short time of instruction can help a group pray with more focus and passion. Or, learning can take place at the end of a time of prayer when the facilitator simply summarizes what God did and how He directed the group. Or he may ask the group what God had spoken to them about. These topics can also help provide further direction in prayer.

One time there were about 20 of us in the room. As I was reflecting how the Lord had led us, I realized we had prayed about the first two of three parts to Psalm 24. Verses 1-2 exalt God as the One who owns everything. We had done that. Verses 3-6 describe those who come to seek the Lord. We had prayed through this as well. The rest of the Psalm is a mighty cry to welcome the King of glory. When I noticed this, I invited the pray-ers to turn to Psalm 24 and we read through it. I pointed out how we had prayed to this point, and invited them to pray prayers that would welcome King Jesus to various parts of their live, ministry and area. This set up a very powerful and focused time of prayer.

As I mentioned previously, oftentimes when the Lord shows me some specific way to pray from my own time in His Word, it is very natural to work that into a time of corporate prayer.

➢ **Blessed by Doing** – As your group is praying, be sensitive for what the Lord may be teaching people through the time of prayer. But be very cautions that neither you, nor someone else, turns the prayer time into a teaching time. Guard the times of prayer.

12.8 What other items (i.e. handouts) can help serve dynamic corporate prayer?

We have already mentioned the primary place Scripture has to play in dynamic corporate prayer. There are some wonderful tools that can be developed from Scripture to assist a group in prayer.

Question 7.2 on *concordance praying* contained some examples of this. Here are a few more.

- A list of various attributes of God with a Scripture reference related to each one can lead to a wonderful time of worship and adoration.
- A list of many names/titles/descriptions of Jesus with references.
- I have been in settings when David Bryant has led a time of prayer around seven key prepositions related to Jesus – pondering Who Jesus is to us, for us, over us, before us, within us, through us, and upon us.
- Paul often uses the phrase "so that" in his prayers for churches. You can see this in Ephesians 1:15-19, 3:14-19, Philippians 1:9-11, Colossians 1:9-12, 1 Thessalonians 3:11-13 and 2 Thessalonians 1:11-12. I have put these prayers in 6 columns of one page and distributed it to pastors. I have asked them to notice the specific ways Paul prayed for the churches he cared about and invited us to do the same. There are many prayer opportunities that can come from a page like this.
- Other passages of Scripture can be used in a similar manner, such as
  - Colossians 1:15-20, Hebrews 1:1-14 and Revelation 1:9-20 on the theme of the majesty of Jesus.
  - Passages (or references) on the cross
  - Passages (or references) on the greatness of God
- An individual chapter such as Isaiah 40 (which contains much about the nature of God) that can be marked up.
- A printout of a specific Psalm can be very helpful. Ps. 24, 84, 89, 107, 145, even 119, can work well for this. Share briefly about the specific theme and invite people to pursue that theme from that Psalm.
- A video such as "That's My King" by Dr. S. M. Lockridge can lead to or cap off a wonderful time of Jesus-focused prayer.
- There are other significant prayers from books that can be read aloud and used as a point of introduction to other prayers.

- Martin Luther's method of praying through the Lord's Prayer can be used in several different ways.

Each of these examples, and so many others that could be listed, can be shared with a group along with some simple, specific instructions. You may want to give the people a little time to process the instructions on their own, before you invite them to pray together based upon the instructions you have given them. You may also need to resist teaching for a lengthy time. With brief instructions, and time to process them, most groups will pick up on your suggestions and have a wonderful time of prayer.

➤ **Blessed by Doing** – Most of these tools are available at the resources tab at www.uandibook.net. You are welcome to download anything there for free and make use of them in your times of prayer.

12.9 How does "What are your prayer requests?" fit into dynamic corporate prayer?

The most common instruction regarding corporate prayer seems to hub around a question like, "What are your prayer requests?" I want to state very clearly that there is nothing wrong with asking this question to find out specific things people have on their hearts to pray for. But I have observed that too often this is the *only* introduction to a time of corporate prayer. My concern is that if this is the only way we introduce a time of prayer, it may cause people to have a faulty view of prayer and of God.

If this is all people hear, it may communicate that the primary purpose of prayer is to get something from God or to have God accomplish something we'd like Him to do. Certainly God invites us to make our requests known to Him, but a far greater purpose of prayer is to know Him, to let Him shape us, form the image of God in us, and let His life affect our life.

And a steady diet of this repeated question can teach us that prayer is primarily about meeting our needs rather than accomplishing His purposes. He certainly is interested in meeting our needs and in addressing the needs we see in our world. But I am convinced that we should also set prayer time aside to pray for His requests and His desires, not just ours.

> *Too often this is the only introduction to a time of corporate prayer.*

This is well illustrated in the two parts of the Lord's Prayer.[29] In the first three requests, the repeated pronoun is "Your" (or "Thy"). It is mentioned three times: Your name, Your kingdom, Your will. In the second part of the prayer, the key pronoun is "us." It is mentioned four times: give us, forgive us, lead us, and deliver us.

There are clearly two kinds of prayer requests mentioned here: those which relate to God and his big desires and those which relate to us and our needs. I suggest that praying for God's everlasting, overarching desires should take precedence over our temporary, specific needs. Again, it is not that we should not pray for the needs we see around us, but rather that we should not forget to pray about God's desire as well. Simply stated, in the specific instructions on prayer that Jesus gave us, He prayed the, "Your" half before He prayed the, "us" half. I believe we should follow a similar pattern.

➤ **Blessed by Doing** – What is your response to the first paragraph of this answer? Do you agree that its continual use could be detrimental? If so, how? If not, why not?

12.9.1 Then how can we pray effectively for other people in this model?

There are several ways we can know and pray for the requests of another without asking them specifically. At certain points during

---

[29] See footnote 1 on page 38.

times of dynamic corporate prayer, it is very appropriate that we pray for one another. As we focus on the Lord and His worth in prayer, often times we will have a greater sense of His love for people and what He desires for them.

- As we are worshiping, when we become aware of a specific action God wants us to take, or part of His deep desire for another person, it can be very appropriate for one person to begin praying for another person. There is something powerful about moving from where you are to stand close to the person you are praying for. Inviting others to pray in a similar way for the same person or a different person can increase the effectiveness of this season of prayer. I have seen the Lord direct people to pray in this manner and the person receiving the prayer is deeply ministered to.

- As people in the group are praying, perhaps someone will pray about a specific need they have or an issue they are facing. It is very right for the facilitator to not only notice this, but to invite others to join that person in lifting that burden to the Lord.

- When someone is praying about a specific need, if the facilitator senses it is a need that others are sharing at that time, he/she may want to invite others to come and stand with the original pray-er identifying with that need. As mentioned above this often happens around the theme of children who are not in good, strong, healthy relationship with the Lord.

- A larger group of people may be invited to get into smaller groups of 5-6 to pray for one another. Like *the chair* ministry described above in Question 12.6 above, this can be a very powerful time of prayer. Asking people to state their request directly to the Lord rather than to share the request works very well because people communicate with Him on a deeper level than they do when they are sharing with others. It also encourages the others to listen well so they know how to pray best for the need. Finally, this is helpful because it allows the group to spend more time in prayer and less time sharing prayer requests which at times can get lengthy and complicated.

- In these smaller settings, you may want to consider asking people to pray for one another from a particular passage of Scripture. The fruit of the Spirit (Galatians 5:22-23) or the Beatitudes (Matthew 5:3-10) or Paul's instructions on living a new life (Ephesians 4:20-32 or the entire chapter of Colossians 3) works well for this. Praying from these and other passages of Scripture are powerful because His Word is powerful. And it is remarkable to see how the Holy Spirit directs prayer when we give Him the opportunity to do so.

➢ **Blessed by Doing** – Pray for the requests of those in your group in a fresh way. Follow one of the suggestions above or one the Lord gives you without using the standard, "What are your prayer requests?" question.

12.9.2 Does dynamic corporate prayer work when we have a specific prayer focus?

As I have advocated throughout this book, it is very valid to come to God without an agenda, only with an open heart, an open Bible, and an open spirit, and see how He would lead us in prayer. And there are also times when a group wants to and should pray on a specific subject. The principles I have mentioned in this book can and should apply to these times as well.

- When a church does a Vacation Bible School and there is a team of people praying before during, and after the VBS, it would be very appropriate for the group to gather and ask Him how they should pray, rather than having one person present the prayer list.

- When a church gathers to pray for the missionaries they support, it would work very well to open to a passage of Scripture and pray for the missionaries based upon that passage. Psalm 67 or 85 would work well for this. Passages from the Gospels (such as the parables in Matthew 13 or John 4:3-42) or the Epistles (such as 1 Thessalonians 1:4-10 or 2:1-13) would also work well. As the leader prays in her/his own personal life, the Lord may lead them to specific section of Scripture that will *pray well* in that setting.

- During pre-service prayer a group can pray through the key points of the pastor's message or for each of the ministry teams that will be functioning during the service.
- If there is a death or serious accident that occurs a group could gather and pray using Lamentations 3:19-26 or 1 Thessalonians 4:13-18 as the basis of their prayers.

Many other examples could be given, but the key idea is to merge Scripture, worship, and the leading of His Spirit together, allowing many (if not all) of the people in the group to participate.

➢ **Blessed by Doing** – When there is a specific event or need that should be prayed about, consider how you may incorporate what you have read in this book into that time of prayer. As it is appropriate, facilitate the prayer that merges Scripture, worship, the leading of the Holy Spirit, and the participation of many into that time of prayer.

United and Ignited

Postlude

If you have worked all the way through this book, if you have read each question and answer, if you have considered what I have written here (whether you agree with it or not), if you have looked at the **Blessed by Doing** sections, and especially if you have put to use what you have read here, you are to be congratulated! In fact, it seems you should be graduated as well. Or at least you should receive a *Certificate of Completion*.

So, I would like us all to rise, please, and direct your attention to the podium.

Now, with the power vested in me, as the author of this book, it gives me great joy to present to you this *Certificate of Comple....*

Wait a minute! I have neither the power nor the opportunity to present anything like that to you! But I know One who does!

So, with the power vested in me, I exhort you to finish the race! I encourage you to complete the journey. I charge you to keep on...

- working at it.
- listening for His voice.
- seeking the Lord simply for who He is.
- spending time in His Word.
- making and taking every opportunity to facilitate dynamic corporate prayer.

Don't give up. Don't be discouraged. Don't *try* to do it, do it.

Then, you will receive the *Certificate of Completion* that really matters, from the One who really matters! You will help others be more effective in one of the two most important spiritual disciplines there are. You will help them love the Lord more. You will help them love others more. You will help disciple them. You will help them be *united*. You will help them be *ignited*.

Then finally, the only One authorized to grant the most significant **Certificate of Completion** anyone can receive will say... "Well done!"

If what I have written here gives you more reasons to hear those wonderful words, I am deeply grateful!

About the Author

Dennis Fuqua (pronounced few-kway) has been the director of International Renewal Ministries since the year 2000 (www.prayersummit.net). Prior to that, he pastored for twenty-five years in Gig Harbor, Washington. In 1989 IRM (under the direction of Dr. Joe Aldrich) gave birth to the Pastors' Prayer Summit movement. Now Dennis helps shepherd this movement, which has spread to at least forty states and over thirty nations. He has had the privilege of facilitating thousands of hours of corporate prayer in multiple-day Prayer Summits, congregations, classrooms, at retreats, and many other settings. These opportunities have given him a unique experience and perspective which he shares in this book. His love for the Written Word and the Living Word has not only helped guide these times of prayer but also his life.

He earned both his Bachelor's and Master's degrees in ministry at Multnomah University, Portland, Oregon.

He speaks often on the topics of individual and corporate prayer in congregations, conferences, classrooms, and retreats. His passion is to see the church relate best to God, itself, and to those who have not yet placed their faith in Jesus Christ. He is a member of America's National Prayer Committee and Mission America Coalition and serves as one of the coaches of their "Loving Our Communities to Christ" process.

His articles have appeared in several magazines including *Pray! Magazine* and *Prayer Connect*.

He is also the author of the 2010 book *Living Prayer: The Lord's Prayer Alive in You* (www.livingprayer.net).

Dennis and his wife, Marilyn, have four adult children and seven grandchildren. They live in Vancouver, Washington.

United and Ignited

Now it's you turn...

If this book has been helpful to you, if it has helped sharpen your prayer desire and skill, if you think others would benefit by its message, if you see how it would help you and others know and love the Savior better, then there are some things you could do to encourage others to get it, read it, and use it.

- Share the book with others. As you read the book, did names come to your mind of people who should read it? If so, encourage them to go to the web site www.uandibook.net and order a copy. Quantity discounts are available.
- Considering ordering copies for them and others as gifts.
- Share it with your pastor or other prayer leaders.
- Mention it or post a brief review of it on your Facebook page.
- Post a review on Amazon or other blogs or web sites. Or submit it to a magazine. And I would love it if you sent me a copy of your review.
- If you would like to have Dennis come share on this topic with your congregation or group, he is an experienced and gifted communicator and would be happy to consider your request. Contact him through the web site or at dennisfuqua@gmail.com.

United and Ignited